Cambridge School
Shakespeare

Twelfth Night

Edited by Rex Gibson

Series Editor: Rex Gibson
Director, Shakespeare and Schools Project

CAMBRIDGE
UNIVERSITY PRESS

CAMBRIDGE UNIVERSITY PRESS
Cambridge, New York, Melbourne, Madrid, Cape Town,
Singapore, São Paulo, Delhi, Mexico City

Cambridge University Press
The Edinburgh Building, Cambridge CB2 8RU, UK

www.cambridge.org
Information on this title: www.cambridge.org/9780521618779

First published 1993
Second edition 2005
9th printing 2012

Printed and bound in the United Kingdom by the MPG Books Group

A catalogue record for this publication is available from the British Library

ISBN   978-0-521-61877-9 Paperback

ACKNOWLEDGEMENTS
Thanks are due to the following for permission to reproduce illustrations:
Cover, vi, vii, viii, ix, x, xi, xii, 8, 22, 44, 84, 118, 125*tl*, 125*tr*, 125*bl*, 150, 155, 159, 161, 163,
171, 177, 178, 179, Donald Cooper/Photostage; v, Jonathan Root; 12, 56, 62, 90, 125*br*,
Morris Newcombe; 35, Zoë Dominic; 38, 138, Tom Holte Theatre Photographic Collec-
tion © Shakespeare Birthplace Trust; 69, Clive Barda; 70, Mary Evans Picture Library;
78, 80, 148, photographer Reg Wilson © Royal Shakespeare Company; 102, Joe Cocks
Studio Collection © Shakespeare Birthplace Trust; 109, Joe Cocks Studio Collection by
permission of the Stratford-upon-Avon Herald; 169, Philip Craven – Robert Harding
World Imagery; 173, Koninklijk Museum voor Schone Kunsten, Antwerp; 175, John
Tramper.

Cover design by Smith

Contents

Cambridge School
Shakespeare

This edition of *Twelfth Night* is part of the **Cambridge School Shakespeare** series. Like every other play in the series, it has been specially prepared to help all students in schools and colleges.

This *Twelfth Night* aims to be different from other editions of the play. It invites you to bring the play to life in your classroom, hall or drama studio through enjoyable activities that will increase your understanding. Actors have created their different interpretations of the play over the centuries. Similarly, you are encouraged to make up your own mind about *Twelfth Night*, rather than having someone else's interpretation handed down to you.

Cambridge School Shakespeare does not offer you a cut-down or simplified version of the play. This is Shakespeare's language, filled with imaginative possibilities. You will find on every left-hand page: a summary of the action, an explanation of unfamiliar words, a choice of activities on Shakespeare's language, characters and stories.

Between each act and in the pages at the end of the play, you will find notes, illustrations and activities. These will help to increase your understanding of the whole play.

There are a large number of activities to give you the widest choice to suit your own particular needs. Please don't think you have to do every one. Choose the activities that will help you most.

This edition will be of value to you whether you are studying for an examination, reading for pleasure, or thinking of putting on the play to entertain others. You can work on the activities on your own or in groups. Many of the activities suggest a particular group size, but don't be afraid to make up larger or smaller groups to suit your own purposes.

Although you are invited to treat *Twelfth Night* as a play, you don't need special dramatic or theatrical skills to do the activities. By choosing your activities, and by exploring and experimenting, you can make your own interpretations of Shakespeare's language, characters and stories. Whatever you do, remember that Shakespeare wrote his plays to be acted, watched and enjoyed.

Rex Gibson

This edition of *Twelfth Night* uses the text of the play established by Elizabeth Story Donno in **The New Cambridge Shakespeare**.

Twins! Viola (left) and Sebastian are shipwrecked off the coast of Illyria. Each thinks the other is drowned. Viola decides to dress as a man and try her fortune at the court of Duke Orsino. And that's where the comedy begins: her disguise results in all kinds of problems of mistaken identity, much to do with love.

'Unfold the passion of my love'. Duke Orsino thinks he is in love with the Countess Olivia, but is really more in love with the idea of love. Viola, disguised as a man and calling herself Cesario, has become Orsino's favourite courtier. He sends her to woo Olivia on his behalf. But she has fallen in love with Orsino!

'I am not what I am'. Olivia has fallen head over heels in love with the disguised Viola, thinking Cesario/Viola to be a man. Viola hopes that time will sort out the problem.

'What a caterwauling do you keep here!' Maria, Olivia's gentlewoman, rebukes Sir Toby Belch (left), Olivia's uncle, Feste, her fool, and Sir Andrew Aguecheek for their drunken singing. Their riotous behaviour brings a much stronger rebuke from Malvolio, Olivia's steward. Sir Toby and Maria plan to humiliate Malvolio, by having him discover a letter seemingly from Olivia, declaring her love for him.

'This wins him, liver and all'. The sober puritan Malvolio has found the forged letter. He reads it and believes that Olivia loves him. He vows to do as instructed: dress in yellow stockings, cross-gartered – and to smile! The conspirators, hiding behind the box hedge, are delighted that their plan has worked.

Malvolio dresses just as the forged letter instructed. But Olivia is perplexed by his appearance and behaviour, thinking it 'midsummer madness'. She orders that Sir Toby take care of Malvolio. But Sir Toby treats Malvolio as a madman and locks him in a dark room to further humiliate him.

'He will not hurt you'. More midsummer madness as Sir Toby forces Sir Andrew to fight a duel with the disguised Viola (see pictures of the duel on pp. 102 and 109). Only more confusion results!

'Are you not mad indeed?' Feste taunts the imprisoned Malvolio.

'Do I stand there?' A moment of wonder as the twins are reunited. Sebastian and Viola discover that they have both survived the shipwreck.

'Let me see thee in thy woman's weeds'. Orsino (centre) switches his love to Viola, as the newly married Sebastian and Olivia look on. All seems resolved, but Malvolio, released from imprisonment, has sworn revenge.

List of characters

Illyria

The Duke's court
ORSINO, Duke of Illyria
VALENTINE, a courtier
CURIO, a courtier
Musicians
Lords
Officers

The Countess's household
OLIVIA, a countess
SIR TOBY BELCH, her uncle
MALVOLIO, her steward
FESTE, her fool
MARIA, her gentlewoman
FABIAN, a servant

A PRIEST
A SEA CAPTAIN

The visitors
VIOLA, later called Cesario
SEBASTIAN, her twin brother
SIR ANDREW AGUECHEEK, suitor to Olivia
ANTONIO, a friend to Sebastian
Sailors

The action of the play takes place in Illyria

Orsino calls for music to feed his hunger for love. He reflects that love is like the sea, absorbing and devaluing every other experience. He claims to be completely obsessed by his love for Olivia.

1 Orsino: in love or infatuated? (in groups of three)

The best approach to Scene 1 is to take parts as Orsino, Curio and Valentine, and read it through. Then change roles and read through again. Don't worry about unfamiliar words in these read-throughs, but afterwards work on the following activities:

a **Love or infatuation?** The opening lines suggest the play will be much about love. But what sort of love? You will find various expressions of love throughout *Twelfth Night*. Many people believe Orsino is not truly in love, but is just infatuated, and wallows in his emotions. To discover your own views, speak lines 1–15 in different ways (e.g. thoughtfully, sadly, pompously). Then talk together about whether you think his language is that of a true lover.

b **The musicians' view of Orsino** In line 4, Orsino asks for a musical refrain to be repeated ('That strain again'). But by line 7 he has heard enough, so he tells the musicians to stop playing. How do you think they feel about their master's quick change of mood? One person reads Orsino's lines, pausing at each punctuation mark. In the pauses, the others, as musicians, comment on what Orsino says.

c **Audience laughter?** Advise the actor playing Orsino how to speak line 7: 'Enough; no more.' Would you wish to make the audience laugh?

d **Staging** How would you present Scene 1 on stage? Write notes on set, costumes, and the general impression you would wish to create of Orsino and his court. What kind of music would you use?

e **Imagery** Lines 9–14 are an elaborate image of love as the sea. See page 164 for more on imagery.

---

surfeiting over-filled
That strain again play that again
validity and pitch high value
falls into abatement is lessened
fancy love

high fantastical intensely imaginative
hart male deer (Orsino puns on 'heart')
pestilence plague
fell savage

Twelfth Night
or What You Will

Act 1 Scene 1
Orsino's palace

Music. Enter ORSINO, *Duke of Illyria,* CURIO, *and other Lords*

ORSINO If music be the food of love, play on;
    Give me excess of it, that surfeiting,
    The appetite may sicken and so die.
    That strain again, it had a dying fall;
    O it came o'er my ear like the sweet sound   5
    That breathes upon a bank of violets,
    Stealing and giving odour. Enough; no more.
    'Tis not so sweet now as it was before.
    O spirit of love, how quick and fresh art thou,
    That, notwithstanding thy capacity,   10
    Receiveth as the sea. Nought enters there,
    Of what validity and pitch soe'er,
    But falls into abatement and low price
    Even in a minute. So full of shapes is fancy,
    That it alone is high fantastical.   15
CURIO Will you go hunt, my lord?
ORSINO   What, Curio?
CURIO The hart.
ORSINO Why so I do, the noblest that I have.
    O when mine eyes did see Olivia first,
    Methought she purged the air of pestilence;   20
    That instant was I turned into a hart,
    And my desires like fell and cruel hounds
    E'er since pursue me.

Enter VALENTINE

    How now, what news from her?

Valentine tells of Olivia's vow to mourn her dead brother for seven years. Orsino says that this reveals how she will love him totally. Viola, landed safely after shipwreck, fears for her brother's life.

---

1 Your first impression of Olivia (in pairs)

Olivia has vowed to become a nun for seven years, not even seeing the sky, to mourn for her brother. Write a few words showing what her decision suggests to you that she is like.

2 Bring out Orsino's vanity (in pairs)

Orsino thinks that if Olivia can go to such lengths just for love of a brother, she will be completely obsessed when she falls in love with him. Orsino sees himself becoming 'one selfsame king' of Olivia's 'sweet perfections', filling her sexual desire, thought and feeling ('liver, brain, and heart').

Imagine lines 33–41 are a mirror. Take turns to speak them, admiring yourself in that 'mirror', combing your hair and preening. Then tell each other what this activity adds to your view of Orsino.

3 Swift scene change

In modern productions of Shakespeare's plays, each scene flows swiftly into the next with no long delay for scene-shifting. Work out how to transfer the audience in imagination from Orsino's palace to the sea-coast in Scene 2. Present your solution as a design or in writing. Can the musicians help your plan?

4 Illyria = Elysium = England?

In lines 3–4, Viola contrasts 'Elysium' (heaven, a peaceful, welcoming place) with 'Illyria', but their names echo each other, suggesting that Illyria may also be a friendly, dreamlike place. Pages 168–71 reveal more about Illyria's likeness to Elysium (it did also exist as a real place – see p. 34), and how it resembles Shakespeare's England!

---

element   sky
seven years' heat   seven summers
a cloistress   a nun secluded from the world
eye-offending brine   bitter tears
season   preserve

fine frame   exquisite form
rich golden shaft   Cupid's arrow of love
bowers   leafy, secluded places
Perchance   (line 5) perhaps
perchance   (line 6) by good fortune

VALENTINE So please my lord, I might not be admitted,
        But from her handmaid do return this answer: 25
        The element itself, till seven years' heat,
        Shall not behold her face at ample view;
        But like a cloistress she will veilèd walk,
        And water once a day her chamber round
        With eye-offending brine; all this to season   30
        A brother's dead love, which she would keep fresh
        And lasting, in her sad remembrance.
ORSINO O she that hath a heart of that fine frame
        To pay this debt of love but to a brother,
        How will she love, when the rich golden shaft   35
        Hath killed the flock of all affections else
        That live in her; when liver, brain, and heart,
        These sovereign thrones, are all supplied and filled
        Her sweet perfections with one selfsame king!
        Away before me to sweet beds of flowers: 40
        Love-thoughts lie rich when canopied with bowers.

Exeunt

Act 1 Scene 2
The sea-coast of Illyria

Enter VIOLA, *a* CAPTAIN, *and Sailors*

VIOLA What country, friends, is this?
CAPTAIN This is Illyria, lady.
VIOLA And what should I do in Illyria?
        My brother, he is in Elysium.
        Perchance he is not drowned: what think you, sailors?   5
CAPTAIN It is perchance that you yourself were saved.
VIOLA O my poor brother! And so perchance may he be.

The Captain reassures Viola that her brother may also have survived the shipwreck. He tells of Orsino's love for Olivia, and says that Olivia's grief for her brother's death has made her a recluse.

1 Imagery: 'Arion on the dolphin's back' (in pairs)

The Captain uses an image from classical mythology. He compares Sebastian's escape from shipwreck with that of Arion, a legendary Greek musician. Arion leapt overboard to escape sailors who wished to murder him. A dolphin, enchanted by Arion's music, carried him safely to shore. The Captain's story gives Viola hope (it also echoes the power of music suggested in Scene 1).

Some stage productions show Sebastian's struggle to survive. Imagine you are directing the play, and want the audience to see what happens to Sebastian. Write how you would present lines 11–17. Line 16 ('hold acquaintance') means that Sebastian kept afloat quite well – like someone holding their own in a conversation.

2 'He was a bachelor then' – why say that? (in pairs)

Suggest possible reasons for Viola's comment about Orsino: 'He was a bachelor then' (line 29). Talk together about what the words might imply about her character. How do you think she speaks the line?

3 'What great ones do, the less will prattle of'

The Captain's words (line 33) anticipate modern-day paparazzi (photographers who specialise in spying on famous people like royalty, pop stars and 'celebrities'). Together with reporters, they supply the pictures and stories which provide millions of 'the less' (ordinary people) with an endless source of rumour and gossip. Make a collection from newspapers and magazines to illustrate the line.

---

driving drifting
provident full of foresight
unfoldeth to encourages
The like of him that he too survived
very late recently

murmur rumour, gossip
abjured rejected, renounced
Till I . . . estate is until the time is ripe to reveal my true identity
compass achieve, bring about
suit advances

CAPTAIN True, madam, and to comfort you with chance,
　　　 Assure yourself, after our ship did split,
　　　 When you, and those poor number saved with you,　　10
　　　 Hung on our driving boat, I saw your brother
　　　 Most provident in peril, bind himself
　　　 (Courage and hope both teaching him the practice)
　　　 To a strong mast that lived upon the sea;
　　　 Where like Arion on the dolphin's back　　15
　　　 I saw him hold acquaintance with the waves
　　　 So long as I could see.
VIOLA For saying so, there's gold.
　　　 Mine own escape unfoldeth to my hope,
　　　 Whereto thy speech serves for authority,　　20
　　　 The like of him. Know'st thou this country?
CAPTAIN Ay, madam, well, for I was bred and born
　　　 Not three hours' travel from this very place.
VIOLA Who governs here?
CAPTAIN A noble duke in nature as in name.　　25
VIOLA What is his name?
CAPTAIN Orsino.
VIOLA Orsino! I have heard my father name him.
　　　 He was a bachelor then.
CAPTAIN And so is now, or was so very late;　　30
　　　 For but a month ago I went from hence,
　　　 And then 'twas fresh in murmur (as you know
　　　 What great ones do, the less will prattle of)
　　　 That he did seek the love of fair Olivia.
VIOLA What's she?　　35
CAPTAIN A virtuous maid, the daughter of a count
　　　 That died some twelvemonth since, then leaving her
　　　 In the protection of his son, her brother,
　　　 Who shortly also died; for whose dear love
　　　 (They say) she hath abjured the sight　　40
　　　 And company of men.
VIOLA 　　　　　　　　　O that I served that lady,
　　　 And might not be delivered to the world
　　　 Till I had made mine own occasion mellow
　　　 What my estate is!
CAPTAIN 　　　　　　　That were hard to compass,
　　　 Because she will admit no kind of suit,　　45
　　　 No, not the duke's.

Viola says that she trusts the Captain. She plans to disguise herself as a man and become an attendant to Orsino. In Scene 3, Sir Toby Belch complains that Olivia's mourning prevents all enjoyment.

1 Appearance versus reality – show it! (in small groups)

In lines 48–9, Viola states one of Shakespeare's favourite themes: you can't judge by appearances. A beautiful appearance may conceal corruption ('nature with a beauteous wall / Doth oft close in pollution'). Much of *Twelfth Night* is about mistaken identity. Work out a tableau (a frozen picture) to illustrate Viola's comment. Each group shows its tableau to the class, 'freezing' for thirty seconds. Talk together about how similar and different the various tableaux are.

This production made Viola's first appearance strikingly dramatic. Write how you would stage her entry. Describe her costume and movements, and how you would show she is of high social status.

Conceal me what I am disguise my true identity
haply appropriately
The form of my intent my purpose
eunuch castrated male servant with a high-pitched voice

allow prove
hap happen
mute dumb servant
By my troth in faith
cousin close relative (in Elizabethan times 'cousin' was loosely used)

VIOLA There is a fair behaviour in thee, captain,
        And though that nature with a beauteous wall
        Doth oft close in pollution, yet of thee
        I well believe thou hast a mind that suits   50
        With this thy fair and outward character.
        I prithee (and I'll pay thee bounteously)
        Conceal me what I am, and be my aid
        For such disguise as haply shall become
        The form of my intent. I'll serve this duke.   55
        Thou shalt present me as an eunuch to him –
        It may be worth thy pains – for I can sing,
        And speak to him in many sorts of music
        That will allow me very worth his service.
        What else may hap, to time I will commit,   60
        Only shape thou thy silence to my wit.
CAPTAIN Be you his eunuch, and your mute I'll be;
        When my tongue blabs, then let mine eyes not see.
VIOLA I thank thee. Lead me on.

Exeunt

Act 1 Scene 3
A room in Olivia's house

Enter SIR TOBY BELCH and MARIA

SIR TOBY What a plague means my niece to take the death of her brother thus? I am sure care's an enemy to life.

MARIA By my troth, Sir Toby, you must come in earlier o'nights. Your cousin, my lady, takes great exceptions to your ill hours.

SIR TOBY Why, let her except, before excepted.   5

MARIA Ay, but you must confine yourself within the modest limits of order.

SIR TOBY Confine? I'll confine myself no finer than I am: these clothes are good enough to drink in, and so be these boots too; and they be not, let them hang themselves in their own straps.   10

Maria warns Sir Toby that his drunkenness will be his downfall. She is scornful of Sir Andrew Aguecheek (a wooer of Olivia), thinking him stupid. Sir Andrew enters and immediately displays his foolishness.

1 The comedy begins – first impressions (in groups of three)

Sir Toby is a great juggler with words, even when he's drunk. His description of Sir Andrew is full of mockery – he says one thing but means something else. Sir Toby calls Sir Andrew 'tall' (courageous), when he probably thinks him cowardly. Other descriptions also had double meanings for Elizabethan audiences:

viol-de-gamboys   a sexual joke: an instrument held between the knees

without book   implies Andrew learnt by heart without understanding

nature   picked up by Maria and turned into 'natural' (idiot)

Castiliano vulgo   'Look solemn' (like a Castilian from Spain), *or* 'Think of all Sir Andrew's money', *or* 'Talk of the devil', *or* 'More Spanish wine!'

Again, the best thing to do with Scene 3 is to take parts as Sir Toby, Maria and Sir Andrew and read through to gain a first impression. Then work on the activity below and on the activities on the following pages. You might decide to learn the lines, rehearse the scene and act it out!

2 What are they like?

Sir Toby   'quaffing and drinking will undo you'

Maria   Olivia's 'chambermaid' (lady companion, gentlewoman)

Sir Andrew   'a foolish knight'

Write two or three sentences about each character telling what you think they are like. Sketch their costumes. As you work through the play, add to your notes as you learn more about each character.

---

quaffing   drunkenness
ducats   gold coins
prodigal   wastrel, spendthrift
viol-de-gamboys   bass viol or viola de gamba
gust   appetite, relish

substractors   slanderers
coistrill   worthless fellow, knave
parish top   whipping top
shrew   small mouse
Accost   greet courteously

MARIA That quaffing and drinking will undo you: I heard my lady talk
of it yesterday and of a foolish knight that you brought in one night
here to be her wooer.

SIR TOBY Who, Sir Andrew Aguecheek?

MARIA Ay, he.   15

SIR TOBY He's as tall a man as any's in Illyria.

MARIA What's that to th'purpose?

SIR TOBY Why, he has three thousand ducats a year.

MARIA Ay, but he'll have but a year in all these ducats. He's a very fool
and a prodigal.   20

SIR TOBY Fie, that you'll say so! He plays o'th'viol-de-gamboys, and
speaks three or four languages word for word without book, and
hath all the good gifts of nature.

MARIA He hath indeed all, most natural: for besides that he's a fool,
he's a great quarreller; and but that he hath the gift of a coward   25
to allay the gust he hath in quarrelling, 'tis thought among the
prudent he would quickly have the gift of a grave.

SIR TOBY By this hand, they are scoundrels and substractors that say
so of him. Who are they?

MARIA They that add, moreover, he's drunk nightly in your company.   30

SIR TOBY With drinking healths to my niece! I'll drink to her as long
as there is a passage in my throat and drink in Illyria; he's a coward
and a coistrill that will not drink to my niece till his brains turn
o'th'toe like a parish top. What, wench! *Castiliano vulgo*: for here
comes Sir Andrew Agueface.   35

Enter SIR ANDREW [AGUECHEEK]

SIR ANDREW Sir Toby Belch! How now, Sir Toby Belch?

SIR TOBY Sweet Sir Andrew!

SIR ANDREW Bless you, fair shrew.

MARIA And you too, sir.

SIR TOBY Accost, Sir Andrew, accost.   40

SIR ANDREW What's that?

SIR TOBY My niece's chambermaid.

SIR ANDREW Good Mistress Accost, I desire better acquaintance.

MARIA My name is Mary, sir.

SIR ANDREW Good Mistress Mary Accost –   45

SIR TOBY You mistake, knight. 'Accost' is front her, board her, woo
her, assail her.

SIR ANDREW By my troth, I would not undertake her in this company.
Is that the meaning of 'accost'?

Maria mocks Sir Andrew, then leaves. Sir Toby jokes crudely about
Sir Andrew's hair, and Andrew repeats that he intends to go home tomorrow
because he is making no progress at all with his wooing of Olivia.

1 Stage business – what does Maria do?

Actors invent actions ('business') to accompany lines 55–60. In one
production, Maria took Sir Andrew's hand and placed it on the
buttery-bar (a ledge for beer tankards). In another, to Sir Andrew's
great embarrassment, she held his hand to her breast. Invent your
own 'business' for these lines, remembering that 'dry' can also mean
'stupid', or 'thirsty', or 'sexually impotent'.

Sir Andrew and Sir Toby in a Royal Shakespeare Company production. In
another production, Sir Andrew was played as surly and aggressive, rather
than merely foolish. Experiment to see how well that view of him would work
by reading his lines aloud in a confident, angry and blustering manner. Decide
whether it suits your impression of Sir Andrew.

And thou let part so   if you let her go
barren   free from foolishness
canary   sweet wine (from the Canary
Islands)
Christian . . . man   average man
great eater of beef   (see p. 170)
Pourquoi   Why?

tongues   languages
flax on a distaff   (see p. 170)
huswife   hussy, prostitute
(Elizabethans believed that sexually
transmitted diseases caused loss of
hair)
hard by   nearby

MARIA Fare you well, gentlemen. [*Leaving*] 50

SIR TOBY And thou let part so, Sir Andrew, would thou mightst never draw sword again.

SIR ANDREW And you part so, mistress, I would I might never draw sword again. Fair lady, do you think you have fools in hand?

MARIA Sir, I have not you by th'hand. 55

SIR ANDREW Marry, but you shall have, and here's my hand.

MARIA Now, sir, thought is free. I pray you bring your hand to th'buttery-bar and let it drink.

SIR ANDREW Wherefore, sweetheart? What's your metaphor?

MARIA It's dry, sir. 60

SIR ANDREW Why, I think so: I am not such an ass but I can keep my hand dry. But what's your jest?

MARIA A dry jest, sir.

SIR ANDREW Are you full of them?

MARIA Ay, sir, I have them at my fingers' ends; marry, now I let go 65
your hand, I am barren. *Exit*

SIR TOBY O knight, thou lack'st a cup of canary. [*Hands him a cup*] When did I see thee so put down?

SIR ANDREW Never in your life, I think, unless you see canary put me down. Methinks sometimes I have no more wit than a Christian 70
or an ordinary man has, but I am a great eater of beef, and I believe that does harm to my wit.

SIR TOBY No question.

SIR ANDREW And I thought that, I'd forswear it. I'll ride home tomorrow, Sir Toby. 75

SIR TOBY *Pourquoi*, my dear knight?

SIR ANDREW What is '*pourquoi*'? Do, or not do? I would I had bestowed that time in the tongues that I have in fencing, dancing, and bear-baiting. O had I but followed the arts!

SIR TOBY Then hadst thou had an excellent head of hair. 80

SIR ANDREW Why, would that have mended my hair?

SIR TOBY Past question, for thou seest it will not curl by nature.

SIR ANDREW But it becomes me well enough, does't not?

SIR TOBY Excellent; it hangs like flax on a distaff; and I hope to see a huswife take thee between her legs and spin it off. 85

SIR ANDREW Faith, I'll home tomorrow, Sir Toby; your niece will not be seen, or if she be, it's four to one, she'll none of me. The count himself here hard by woos her.

Sir Toby quickly persuades Sir Andrew to stay, assuring him that Orsino will not marry Olivia. Sir Andrew boasts about his dancing skills, and Sir Toby encourages him to perform – but he capers to Toby's tune.

1 Sir Toby tricks Sir Andrew (in pairs)

a **Success with Olivia** In only three lines (lines 89–91), Sir Toby cunningly persuades Sir Andrew, a gullible ninny, to stay in Illyria. Just how does he do it? Experiment with ways of speaking the lines, making each word or phrase as persuasive as possible. You have to make Sir Andrew believe that he really does have a strong chance of marrying Olivia.

b **Cutting a caper** Sir Toby encourages the foolish Sir Andrew to dance, naming popular dances of the day: 'galliard', a lively dance in triple time; 'coranto', a rapid, running dance; 'jig', a jerky, bouncy dance; 'sink-a-pace', a dance with five steps (Sir Toby can't resist a rude joke: 'make water' = to urinate). Take turns to say lines 102–8 to each other, demonstrating each dance. Remember, your intention is to get Sir Andrew to leap about, so make sure he can't resist your powerful invitation!

2 Opportunities for your imagination!

a Line 100: no one knows what 'the back-trick' is. Invent it!

b Line 103: 'Mistress Mall' might be Maria in the play, or an attendant to Queen Elizabeth I, or an Elizabethan female thief. Imagine you have been invited to give a learned lecture to a conference of Shakespeare scholars and historians on 'Mistress Mall's picture'. Write your lecture and deliver it. Make it all up!

---

match   marry
degree   rank
estate   fortune, wealth
there's life in't   while there's life, there's hope
masques and revels   theatricals (with masks) and dances

kickshawses   trifles (from the French words *quelque chose* meaning 'something')
cut a caper   leap (or spice for mutton)
mutton   meat (or prostitute)
dun-coloured stock   mouse-coloured stocking
Taurus   the bull, a sign of the zodiac

SIR TOBY She'll none o'th'count; she'll not match above her degree, neither in estate, years, nor wit. I have heard her swear't. Tut, there's life in't, man.   90

SIR ANDREW I'll stay a month longer. I am a fellow o'th'strangest mind i'th'world: I delight in masques and revels sometimes altogether.

SIR TOBY Art thou good at these kickshawses, knight?

SIR ANDREW As any man in Illyria, whatsoever he be, under the degree   95 of my betters, and yet I will not compare with an old man.

SIR TOBY What is thy excellence in a galliard, knight?

SIR ANDREW Faith, I can cut a caper.

SIR TOBY And I can cut the mutton to't.

SIR ANDREW And I think I have the back-trick simply as strong as any   100 man in Illyria.

SIR TOBY Wherefore are these things hid? Wherefore have these gifts a curtain before 'em? Are they like to take dust, like Mistress Mall's picture? Why dost thou not go to church in a galliard and come home in a coranto? My very walk should be a jig; I would not so   105 much as make water but in a sink-a-pace. What dost thou mean? Is it a world to hide virtues in? I did think, by the excellent constitution of thy leg, it was formed under the star of a galliard.

SIR ANDREW Ay, 'tis strong, and it does indifferent well in a dun-coloured stock. Shall we set about some revels?   110

SIR TOBY What shall we do else? Were we not born under Taurus?

SIR ANDREW Taurus? That's sides and heart.

SIR TOBY No, sir, it is legs and thighs. Let me see thee caper. Ha, higher; ha, ha, excellent!

Exeunt

Viola, disguised as Cesario, a page, has won the favour of Orsino. He has told her all his secrets. Now Orsino instructs Viola-Cesario to visit Olivia on his behalf to tell her of the strength of his love.

1 The new man – a cuckoo in the nest? (in pairs)

What does Valentine think of Viola-Cesario? This new 'man' has only been at court for three days, but is already highly favoured by Orsino. Take parts and read lines 1–8, experimenting with different tones for Valentine (e.g. jealous, angry, superior, indifferent, mocking, friendly). Which tone do you prefer, and why?

Afterwards, discuss Valentine's reactions when he, with Curio and the others, is ordered to 'Stand you awhile aloof'.

2 Improvise the job interview (in groups of three)

How did Viola gain the post as page to Orsino? Improvise the missing scene in which the Captain presents her (as Cesario) to Orsino. The duke will question her closely about her past, so Viola-Cesario may have written notes for herself about what to say, and how to behave. Write her notes.

3 Orsino's language – heightened and elaborate (in pairs)

Shakespeare gives Orsino a heightened manner of speech. For example, he says 'address thy gait unto her', a showy, ornate way of telling Viola-Cesario to visit Olivia. Try to express something of Orsino's style by taking parts and reading aloud lines 9–41. Orsino should deliberately exaggerate all the words and phrases which you think are affected and self-important.

Change roles and repeat the activity. Then talk together about how you would describe Orsino's language, and what it suggests to you about his personality.

---

much advanced promoted
humour moodiness, changeability
aloof apart
gait steps
leap all civil bounds don't stand on ceremony, be impolite

discourse story
nuncio messenger
grave aspect serious appearance (This probably refers to Valentine. Overhearing it, how does he react?)

Act 1 Scene 4
Orsino's palace

Enter VALENTINE, *and* VIOLA *in man's attire*

VALENTINE If the duke continue these favours towards you, Cesario,
you are like to be much advanced; he hath known you but three
days, and already you are no stranger.

VIOLA You either fear his humour, or my negligence, that you call in
question the continuance of his love. Is he inconstant, sir, in his   5
favours?

VALENTINE No, believe me.

VIOLA I thank you. Here comes the count.

Enter DUKE [ORSINO], CURIO, *and Attendants*

ORSINO Who saw Cesario, ho?

VIOLA On your attendance, my lord, here.   10

ORSINO [*To Curio and Attendants*] Stand you awhile aloof. Cesario,
  Thou know'st no less but all: I have unclasped
  To thee the book even of my secret soul.
  Therefore, good youth, address thy gait unto her,
  Be not denied access; stand at her doors,   15
  And tell them there thy fixèd foot shall grow
  Till thou have audience.

VIOLA   Sure, my noble lord,
  If she be so abandoned to her sorrow
  As it is spoke, she never will admit me.

ORSINO Be clamorous, and leap all civil bounds,   20
  Rather than make unprofited return.

VIOLA Say I do speak with her, my lord, what then?

ORSINO O then unfold the passion of my love,
  Surprise her with discourse of my dear faith;
  It shall become thee well to act my woes: 25
  She will attend it better in thy youth
  Than in a nuncio's of more grave aspect.

Orsino praises the disguised Viola's feminine appearance. Viola reveals (in an Aside) that she loves Orsino. In Scene 5, Feste won't take Maria seriously when she tells him he's in trouble.

---

1 Dramatic irony – Orsino does not know! (in pairs)

Scene 4 is rich in dramatic irony (where the audience knows something that a character on stage does not know). Orsino does not know that he is speaking to a female when he praises Cesario, saying how like a woman 'he' looks. For Shakespeare's audience the irony was intensified, because at that time only males were allowed to act. So Viola-Cesario was a boy, playing a girl, playing a boy!

How do you think Viola-Cesario should react to lines 28–33? One person reads, the other tries out various reactions. For example, if she winked at the audience, would that be out of character?

2 What *does* she see in him?

The sensible, witty Viola has fallen in love with Orsino (line 41). It seems to have been love at first sight. Write a paragraph suggesting what you think Viola sees in Orsino to make her love him.

3 Puns and wordplay: beware of over-explanation!

Feste begins with a pun: dead men see no 'colours' (collars or hangmen's nooses), so they don't fear them. Maria also puns on 'colours' (military flags). The Elizabethans enjoyed such punning jokes, in which words that sound the same have different meanings (see p. 167). Puns are still popular today, but some of the wordplay humour in *Twelfth Night* is not clear to a modern audience or reader. The following pages explain some of this wordplay, hopefully helping you to enjoy the jokes without killing them stone dead in the process!

---

belie mistake
Diana the moon goddess (associated with love)
rubious ruby-red
pipe voice
is semblative resembles

constellation destiny foretold by the stars (see p. 35)
barful obstacle-filled
Make that good prove it
good lenten answer weak joke (like a simple meal in Lent)

VIOLA I think not so, my lord.

ORSINO Dear lad, believe it;
    For they shall yet belie thy happy years
    That say thou art a man: Diana's lip   30
    Is not more smooth and rubious; thy small pipe
    Is as the maiden's organ, shrill and sound,
    And all is semblative a woman's part.
    I know thy constellation is right apt
    For this affair. Some four or five attend him –   35
    All if you will, for I myself am best
    When least in company. Prosper well in this,
    And thou shalt live as freely as thy lord
    To call his fortunes thine.

VIOLA   I'll do my best
    To woo your lady. [*Aside*] Yet a barful strife!   40
    Whoe'er I woo, myself would be his wife.

                Exeunt

Act 1 Scene 5
Olivia's house

Enter MARIA and FESTE

MARIA Nay, either tell me where thou hast been, or I will not open my
lips so wide as a bristle may enter in way of thy excuse. My lady
will hang thee for thy absence.

FESTE Let her hang me: he that is well hanged in this world needs to
fear no colours.   5

MARIA Make that good.

FESTE He shall see none to fear.

MARIA A good lenten answer. I can tell thee where that saying was born,
of 'I fear no colours.'

FESTE Where, good Mistress Mary?   10

MARIA In the wars, and that may you be bold to say in your foolery.

FESTE Well, God give them wisdom that have it; and those that are
fools, let them use their talents.

Feste continues to joke with Maria. He hints that she is in a relationship with Sir Toby. Olivia orders Feste to leave, but he challenges her by offering to prove she is a fool.

---

1 Repartee – make it funny (in pairs)

Maria and Feste are like a comedy duo, scoring points off each other in quick-fire exchanges (repartee). Take parts and read lines 1–26 as a pair of stand-up comedians on television or in a music hall. Use gestures and expressions to add to the humour.

2 'This simple syllogism'

A syllogism is a logical argument which moves carefully from one point to the next. Feste mocks this philosophical method of reasoning in lines 35–43, but, as usual, there is some sense in what he says. Imagine the actor playing Feste says to you: 'I want to play the lines like a philosophy teacher proving an argument. How can I do it? What tone, gestures and props are needed?' Write notes to help him.

3 Feste: the fool – but not foolish

Don't think that because Feste is called the fool, he is foolish. He is always playing with words, and occasionally seems to talk nonsense (for instance, when he invents an imaginary philosopher, Quinapalus). But there's often a lot of truth in what he says. Feste reminds Olivia that he has all his wits about him: 'I wear not motley in my brain'. His Latin quotation *cucullus non facit monachum* (the hood does not make the monk) is yet another reminder of a major theme of the play, appearance versus reality: don't judge by outward appearances.

As you read on, keep thinking about what kind of fool Feste is. You'll find he's a very complex character (see p. 160).

---

to be turned away   dismissed, sacked
points   matters or laces (a pun)
gaskins   wide breeches held up with laces ('points')
Eve's flesh   womanhood
madonna   my lady

botcher   mender of old clothes
syllogism   argument
cuckold   deceived husband
Misprision   error
motley   a fool's clothes (see p. 70)
Dexteriously   skilfully

MARIA Yet you will be hanged for being so long absent – or to be turned
    away: is not that as good as a hanging to you?   15

FESTE Many a good hanging prevents a bad marriage; and for turning
    away, let summer bear it out.

MARIA You are resolute then?

FESTE Not so neither, but I am resolved on two points –

MARIA That if one break, the other will hold, or if both break, your   20
    gaskins fall.

FESTE Apt, in good faith, very apt. Well, go thy way; if Sir Toby would
    leave drinking, thou wert as witty a piece of Eve's flesh as any in
    Illyria.

MARIA Peace, you rogue, no more o'that; here comes my lady: make   25
    your excuse wisely, you were best.   *[Exit]*

         Enter LADY OLIVIA *[attended,] with* MALVOLIO

FESTE Wit, and't be thy will, put me into good fooling! Those wits that
    think they have thee do very oft prove fools, and I that am sure I
    lack thee may pass for a wise man. For what says Quinapalus?
    'Better a witty fool than a foolish wit' – God bless thee, lady.   30

OLIVIA Take the fool away.

FESTE Do you not hear, fellows? Take away the lady.

OLIVIA Go to, y'are a dry fool: I'll no more of you; besides, you grow
    dishonest.

FESTE Two faults, madonna, that drink and good counsel will amend: 35
    for give the dry fool drink, then is the fool not dry; bid the dishonest
    man mend himself; if he mend, he is no longer dishonest; if he
    cannot, let the botcher mend him. Anything that's mended is but
    patched: virtue that transgresses is but patched with sin, and sin
    that amends is but patched with virtue. If that this simple syllogism   40
    will serve, so; if it will not, what remedy? As there is no true cuckold
    but calamity, so beauty's a flower. The lady bade take away the fool;
    therefore I say again, take her away.

OLIVIA Sir, I bade them take away you.

FESTE Misprision in the highest degree! Lady, *cucullus non facit*   45
    monachum: that's as much to say as I wear not motley in my brain.
    Good madonna, give me leave to prove you a fool.

OLIVIA Can you do it?

FESTE Dexteriously, good madonna.

OLIVIA Make your proof.   50

Feste 'proves' Olivia to be a fool, but is treated with contempt by Malvolio. Olivia criticises Malvolio's sour attitude, urging greater charity and generosity of spirit. Maria tells of a visitor.

Malvolio (right) looks on disapprovingly as Feste 'catechises' Olivia.

1 Olivia and Malvolio: contrasts in spirit (in pairs)

Malvolio doesn't just criticise Feste, he also patronises Olivia. The first and last sentences in lines 67–72 are barbed criticisms of Olivia and her dead father. Olivia does not behave like someone who has vowed to shut herself away for seven years. She seems amused by Feste's joking, and she urges Malvolio to show more generosity of spirit. Take parts and experiment with different ways of speaking lines 67–78. Try Malvolio as sneering, or pompous, or deadly serious. Try Olivia as gentle, or sharply critical, or mildly reproving.

---

catechise question
bide await
mend get better (but Malvolio interprets it as 'get worse')
no fox not cunning
crow laugh uproariously
zanies foolish assistants
distempered unwholesome

bird-bolts blunt arrows
allowed licensed, free to speak his mind (see p. 160)
rail reproach, mock
Mercury god of deceit
endue thee with leasing teach you to lie

FESTE I must catechise you for it, madonna. Good my mouse of virtue,
answer me.

OLIVIA Well, sir, for want of other idleness, I'll bide your proof.

FESTE Good madonna, why mourn'st thou?

OLIVIA Good fool, for my brother's death.   55

FESTE I think his soul is in hell, madonna.

OLIVIA I know his soul is in heaven, fool.

FESTE The more fool, madonna, to mourn for your brother's soul being
in heaven. Take away the fool, gentlemen.

OLIVIA What think you of this fool, Malvolio? Doth he not mend?   60

MALVOLIO Yes, and shall do, till the pangs of death shake him;
infirmity, that decays the wise, doth ever make the better fool.

FESTE God send you, sir, a speedy infirmity, for the better increasing
your folly! Sir Toby will be sworn that I am no fox, but he will
not pass his word for twopence that you are no fool.   65

OLIVIA How say you to that, Malvolio?

MALVOLIO I marvel your ladyship takes delight in such a barren rascal.
I saw him put down the other day with an ordinary fool that has
no more brain than a stone. Look you now, he's out of his guard
already. Unless you laugh and minister occasion to him, he is   70
gagged. I protest I take these wise men that crow so at these set
kind of fools no better than the fools' zanies.

OLIVIA O you are sick of self-love, Malvolio, and taste with a
distempered appetite. To be generous, guiltless, and of free
disposition is to take those things for bird-bolts that you deem   75
cannon bullets. There is no slander in an allowed fool though he
do nothing but rail; nor no railing in a known discreet man though
he do nothing but reprove.

FESTE Now Mercury endue thee with leasing, for thou speak'st well
of fools!   80

Enter MARIA

MARIA Madam, there is at the gate a young gentleman much desires
to speak with you.

OLIVIA From the Count Orsino, is it?

MARIA I know not, madam; 'tis a fair young man and well attended.

OLIVIA Who of my people hold him in delay?   85

MARIA Sir Toby, madam, your kinsman.

Olivia sends Malvolio to dismiss the visitor. Sir Toby, who is drunk, muddles his words – or makes a sexual pun. Malvolio returns to explain that the visitor insists on speaking to Olivia.

1 Playing a drunk (in groups of three)

It's very difficult to play the part of a drunken man convincingly. Can you do it? Take turns to play Sir Toby, Feste and Olivia, and act out lines 96–106. Here are two actors' tips for imitating a drunk:

> Imagine your left foot is nailed to the floor. Try to walk in all directions with the other.

> Drunks have problems with speaking and hearing. They misunderstand, like Sir Toby who confuses 'lethargy' and 'lechery'. Struggle with your words, but remember you have to make them perfectly clear to the audience, even if you slur them. So, take your time and search slowly for each word in your mind, as if you are having difficulty finding them.

2 It's a comedy – a chance to write as Shakespeare!

Twice in the lines opposite Shakespeare may be reminding you not to take *Twelfth Night* too seriously, but just to enjoy it as a comedy:

- Line 90 contains the subtitle of the play: 'what you will' (whatever you like). The saying was in common use in Shakespeare's time.
- Sir Toby's line 106 ('Well, it's all one') is the Elizabethan equivalent of 'Whatever', or 'So what?', or 'I couldn't care less'. The expression is used several times in the play, and echoes the subtitle.

Step into role as William Shakespeare. You have been told that *Twelfth Night* is now studied for examinations, and that scholarly books are written on it. Write your response to that news.

---

suit message of love
old stale, not funny
Jove king of the gods (see p. 165)
pia mater brain
pickle herring (Belch belches)
sot drunk

lethargy sleepiness
one draught above heat the first warm drink
crowner coroner
sit o'my coz hold an inquest on my cousin
look to look after

OLIVIA Fetch him off, I pray you; he speaks nothing but madman. Fie
on him.

[*Exit Maria*]

Go you, Malvolio. If it be a suit from the count, I am sick, or not
at home – what you will to dismiss it.   90

Exit Malvolio

Now you see, sir, how your fooling grows old, and people dislike
it.

FESTE Thou hast spoke for us, madonna, as if thy eldest son should be
a fool: whose skull Jove cram with brains, for – here he comes –

Enter SIR TOBY [*staggering*]

one of thy kin has a most weak *pia mater*.   95

OLIVIA By mine honour, half drunk! What is he at the gate, cousin?

SIR TOBY A gentleman.

OLIVIA A gentleman? What gentleman?

SIR TOBY 'Tis a gentleman here – [*Hiccuping*] a plague o'these pickle
herring! How now, sot?   100

FESTE Good Sir Toby –

OLIVIA Cousin, cousin, how have you come so early by this lethargy?

SIR TOBY Lechery! I defy lechery. There's one at the gate.

OLIVIA Ay, marry, what is he?

SIR TOBY Let him be the devil and he will, I care not: give me faith,   105
say I. Well, it's all one.   *Exit*

OLIVIA What's a drunken man like, fool?

FESTE Like a drowned man, a fool, and a madman: one draught above
heat makes him a fool, the second mads him, and a third drowns
him.   110

OLIVIA Go thou and seek the crowner, and let him sit o'my coz, for
he's in the third degree of drink: he's drowned. Go look after him.

FESTE He is but mad yet, madonna, and the fool shall look to the
madman.   [*Exit*]

Enter MALVOLIO

MALVOLIO Madam, yond young fellow swears he will speak with you.   115
I told him you were sick; he takes on him to understand so much
and therefore comes to speak with you. I told him you were asleep;
he seems to have a foreknowledge of that too, and therefore comes
to speak with you. What is to be said to him, lady? He's fortified
against any denial.   120

Malvolio haughtily describes Viola's appearance as sexually ambiguous. Olivia commands Maria to veil her. Viola enters (disguised as Cesario) and seeks to discover which woman is Olivia.

___

1 Catch Malvolio's tone (in pairs)

In Malvolio's disdainful description of Viola-Cesario (lines 130–4), which is full of comparisons, he likens 'him' to an unripe apple ('codling'/'apple'), and to the time when the tide turns ('in standing water'). To catch his haughty tone, pinch your nose between forefinger and thumb, lean your head back, and speak the lines slowly, pausing after every punctuation mark. Listen to the note of superiority, condescension and disdain in your voice. Ask each other: 'Is that how Malvolio speaks?'

2 Viola-Cesario's high-flown speech of love

Viola-Cesario begins her address to Olivia in high style: 'Most radiant, exquisite, and unmatchable beauty'. But she is disconcerted by not knowing if it is really Olivia she is speaking to. She never gets to finish the elaborate speech she has so carefully prepared, or which Orsino may well have written for her. Write the next few lines of her prepared speech to follow on from her high-sounding opening words.

3 Acting a part – make them laugh

In lines 141–54 Shakespeare includes references to the theatre: 'speech', 'well penned', 'con' (learn by heart), 'studied', 'part', 'comedian' (actor), 'play'. You will find other mentions of acting as you read on (and see p. 156).

Viola says 'I am not that I play' (line 153). What advice (on expression, gesture and tone) would you give to the actor playing Viola to help her make the audience laugh at this line?

___

sheriff's post post outside a sheriff's door (for notices)
supporter to a bench prop
squash unripe peapod
peascod peapod
codling unripe apple
shrewishly sharply
cast away waste
comptible sensitive
least sinister usage slightest discourtesy
comedian actor (The meaning has changed since Shakespeare's time!)
usurp betray

OLIVIA Tell him he shall not speak with me.

MALVOLIO H'as been told so; and he says he'll stand at your door like a sheriff's post, and be the supporter to a bench, but he'll speak with you.

OLIVIA What kind o'man is he? 125

MALVOLIO Why, of mankind.

OLIVIA What manner of man?

MALVOLIO Of very ill manner: he'll speak with you, will you or no.

OLIVIA Of what personage and years is he?

MALVOLIO Not yet old enough for a man, nor young enough for a boy: 130 as a squash is before 'tis a peascod, or a codling when 'tis almost an apple. 'Tis with him in standing water, between boy and man. He is very well-favoured and he speaks very shrewishly. One would think his mother's milk were scarce out of him.

OLIVIA Let him approach. Call in my gentlewoman. 135

MALVOLIO Gentlewoman, my lady calls. *Exit*

Enter MARIA

OLIVIA Give me my veil; come throw it o'er my face.
We'll once more hear Orsino's embassy.

Enter VIOLA

VIOLA The honourable lady of the house, which is she?

OLIVIA Speak to me; I shall answer for her. Your will? 140

VIOLA Most radiant, exquisite, and unmatchable beauty – I pray you tell me if this be the lady of the house, for I never saw her. I would be loath to cast away my speech: for besides that it is excellently well penned, I have taken great pains to con it. Good beauties, let me sustain no scorn; I am very comptible, even to the least sinister 145 usage.

OLIVIA Whence came you, sir?

VIOLA I can say little more than I have studied, and that question's out of my part. Good gentle one, give me modest assurance if you be the lady of the house, that I may proceed in my speech. 150

OLIVIA Are you a comedian?

VIOLA No, my profound heart; and yet, by the very fangs of malice, I swear, I am not that I play. Are you the lady of the house?

OLIVIA If I do not usurp myself, I am.

After some verbal fencing, Viola says her message is for Olivia alone. Maria is dismissed. Olivia playfully questions Viola, who asks to see her face. Olivia unveils.

1 Unfamiliar expressions – help the audience

Shakespeare's audiences were more familiar with certain expressions than we are today (see p. 170). Suggest how an actor could help a modern audience understand each of the following phrases:

Lines 164–5 ''Tis not that time of moon with me to make one in so skipping a dialogue' (the moon was thought to bring on lunacy)

Line 173 'taxation of homage' (a demand for submission and loyalty)

Line 180 'What is your text?' (Olivia begins questioning Viola as though conducting a catechism – an examination by a series of questions)

Line 186 'To answer by the method' (to make the reply in the appropriate style in this catechism you are putting me through)

Lines 191–2 'such a one I was this present' (here's a portrait of me now).

2 Olivia's growing interest – and her unveiling (in pairs)

Olivia has vowed to mourn her dead brother and to avoid men for seven years. But she responds in a very positive way to Viola-Cesario's liveliness. At line 191 she unveils her face. This is a very significant gesture. It suggests that her thoughts and feelings are very far from being sad ones. Olivia has evidently become fascinated by the appearance and language of Viola-Cesario.

Talk together about just where in the script you think Olivia begins to be attracted by Viola-Cesario. Write notes on how you would stage the encounter to show Olivia's growing fascination. And might she unveil flirtatiously, fishing for a compliment?

usurp wrong (by withholding from marriage)
from my commission not part of my instructions
feigned pretended
make one in join in
swabber deck-cleaner, sailor
hull float, stay
mollification calming down, appeasement
the olive olive branch of peace
entertainment reception
maidenhead virginity
by the method in the style
heresy false doctrine, contrary belief

VIOLA Most certain, if you are she, you do usurp yourself: for what is   155
yours to bestow is not yours to reserve. But this is from my
commission. I will on with my speech in your praise, and then show
you the heart of my message.

OLIVIA Come to what is important in't: I forgive you the praise.

VIOLA Alas, I took great pains to study it, and 'tis poetical.   160

OLIVIA It is the more like to be feigned; I pray you keep it in. I heard
you were saucy at my gates, and allowed your approach rather to
wonder at you than to hear you. If you be not mad, be gone; if
you have reason, be brief. 'Tis not that time of moon with me to
make one in so skipping a dialogue.   165

MARIA Will you hoist sail, sir? Here lies your way.

VIOLA No, good swabber, I am to hull here a little longer. Some
mollification for your giant, sweet lady! Tell me your mind, I am
a messenger.

OLIVIA Sure you have some hideous matter to deliver, when the   170
courtesy of it is so fearful. Speak your office.

VIOLA It alone concerns your ear. I bring no overture of war, no
taxation of homage; I hold the olive in my hand; my words are as
full of peace as matter.

OLIVIA Yet you began rudely. What are you? What would you?   175

VIOLA The rudeness that hath appeared in me I learned from my
entertainment. What I am, and what I would, are as secret as
maidenhead: to your ears, divinity; to any other's, profanation.

OLIVIA Give us the place alone; we will hear this divinity.
                    [*Exeunt Maria and Attendants*]
Now, sir, what is your text?   180

VIOLA Most sweet lady –

OLIVIA A comfortable doctrine, and much may be said of it. Where lies
your text?

VIOLA In Orsino's bosom.

OLIVIA In his bosom? In what chapter of his bosom?   185

VIOLA To answer by the method, in the first of his heart.

OLIVIA O I have read it. It is heresy. Have you no more to say?

VIOLA Good madam, let me see your face.

OLIVIA Have you any commission from your lord to negotiate with my
face? You are now out of your text, but we will draw the curtain   190
and show you the picture. [*Unveiling*] Look you, sir, such a one I
was this present. Is't not well done?

Viola accuses Olivia of keeping her beauty to herself by not having children. Olivia replies mockingly. Viola explains that if she were the one who loved Olivia, every action would express her love and move Olivia to pity her.

1 Have 'copy' (children) – OK, I'll leave a list! (in pairs)

In lines 197–9, Viola appeals to Olivia to marry and have children ('copy'). In this way, Olivia can ensure that her beauty is handed on and kept alive in the world after her death. Viola's plea echoes the theme of the first seventeen of Shakespeare's *Sonnets*. But Olivia mocks Viola by taking 'copy' literally. She proposes to leave various lists ('divers schedules') itemising all the elements of her beauty.

Take parts and read lines 197–204. Play Viola as sincere and reproving. Make Olivia's response mocking and teasing.

2 Orsino's qualities – show them (in small groups)

Olivia lists at least nine of Orsino's qualities in lines 213–17. Identify his various qualities, then prepare a series of tableaux (frozen pictures) to show each one ('virtuous', 'noble', etc.). Present your version to the class. Can other groups guess each of Orsino's qualities that you show?

3 'Make me a willow cabin at your gate' (in small groups)

Lines 223–31 contain some of Shakespeare's best-known love poetry. Work out a group presentation of the lines that is dramatically effective. You could use choral speaking, or share out the lines, or add sound effects or mimes, or sing the lines, or echo particular words and phrases (the 'willow' was an emblem of sorrowful love; 'cantons' are songs; 'contemnèd' means 'rejected' or 'despised'; 'Hallow' means 'shout' and 'babbling gossip' means 'echo').

---

in grain natural, indelible
blent blended
divers schedules various lists
inventoried classified
'praise value, appraise
Could be but recompensed would receive no more than its due reward

nonpareil incomparable, unequalled
great estate very high status
In voices well divulged well spoken of, high reputation
flame passion
reverberate echoing

VIOLA Excellently done, if God did all.

OLIVIA 'Tis in grain, sir; 'twill endure wind and weather.

VIOLA 'Tis beauty truly blent, whose red and white   195
　　　Nature's own sweet and cunning hand laid on.
　　　Lady, you are the cruell'st she alive,
　　　If you will lead these graces to the grave,
　　　And leave the world no copy.

OLIVIA O sir, I will not be so hard-hearted: I will give out divers   200
schedules of my beauty. It shall be inventoried and every particle
and utensil labelled to my will, as, *item*, two lips, indifferent red;
item, two grey eyes, with lids to them; *item*, one neck, one chin,
and so forth. Were you sent hither to 'praise me?

VIOLA I see you what you are. You are too proud;   205
　　　But if you were the devil, you are fair!
　　　My lord and master loves you. O such love
　　　Could be but recompensed, though you were crowned
　　　The nonpareil of beauty.

OLIVIA　　　　　　　　How does he love me?

VIOLA With adorations, fertile tears,   210
　　　With groans that thunder love, with sighs of fire.

OLIVIA Your lord does know my mind. I cannot love him.
　　　Yet I suppose him virtuous, know him noble,
　　　Of great estate, of fresh and stainless youth;
　　　In voices well divulged, free, learned, and valiant,   215
　　　And in dimension, and the shape of nature,
　　　A gracious person. But yet I cannot love him.
　　　He might have took his answer long ago.

VIOLA If I did love you in my master's flame,
　　　With such a suff'ring, such a deadly life,   220
　　　In your denial I would find no sense;
　　　I would not understand it.

OLIVIA　　　　　　　　Why, what would you?

VIOLA Make me a willow cabin at your gate,
　　　And call upon my soul within the house;
　　　Write loyal cantons of contemnèd love,   225
　　　And sing them loud even in the dead of night;
　　　Hallow your name to the reverberate hills,
　　　And make the babbling gossip of the air
　　　Cry out 'Olivia!' O you should not rest
　　　Between the elements of air and earth   230
　　　But you should pity me!

Viola rejects payment. She leaves, wishing that Olivia, like Orsino, may suffer from rejected love. Olivia fears that she is falling in love with Viola-Cesario. She sends Malvolio on a false errand to ensure that Viola returns.

---

1 Love strikes! How does Olivia respond?

Viola-Cesario's 'willow cabin' speech has bewitched Olivia. She is now well and truly in love with this attractive young man. Her initial response is just four words in line 231: 'You might do much.' But how does she speak those words? In some performances, she pauses a long time, then says them wonderingly, then pulls herself together to ask, 'What is your parentage?' Write a paragraph on how Olivia responds throughout the 'willow cabin' speech, and how she speaks her four words.

2 Can you judge by appearances? (in pairs)

Olivia judges Viola-Cesario to be a 'gentleman' by five qualities ('five-fold blazon', line 248): speech, looks, body, behaviour and spirit. But at line 264, Olivia fears that she may have been deceived by appearances: 'Mine eye too great a flatterer for my mind'. Certainly, she has been deceived by Viola-Cesario's outward appearance.

a Can you judge someone's true quality by their appearance? Could you recognise a prince even if he were dressed in rags?

b Discuss each of the five qualities (line 247) in turn, and decide if you think they are a reliable guide to character.

3 'What is decreed must be' – really? (in small groups)

Talk together about line 266. Do you agree with Olivia that 'Fate' determines a person's love life? Page 35 has more on the influence of 'the stars'.

---

fortunes present social status	**catch the plague** fall in love
my state is well I'm content	**peevish** irritating
fee'd post paid messenger	**county's** Count Orsino's
fervour passionate love	**Hie thee** Make haste!
blazon coat of arms, marks of gentility	**owe** own

OLIVIA   You might do much.
          What is your parentage?
VIOLA Above my fortunes, yet my state is well:
          I am a gentleman.
OLIVIA   Get you to your lord.
          I cannot love him. Let him send no more –   235
          Unless (perchance) you come to me again,
          To tell me how he takes it. Fare you well.
          I thank you for your pains. Spend this for me.
VIOLA I am no fee'd post, lady; keep your purse;
          My master, not myself, lacks recompense.   240
          Love make his heart of flint that you shall love,
          And let your fervour like my master's be
          Placed in contempt. Farewell, fair cruelty.   *Exit*
OLIVIA 'What is your parentage?'
          'Above my fortunes, yet my state is well: 245
          I am a gentleman.' I'll be sworn thou art;
          Thy tongue, thy face, thy limbs, actions, and spirit
          Do give thee five-fold blazon. Not too fast! Soft, soft!
          Unless the master were the man – How now?
          Even so quickly may one catch the plague?   250
          Methinks I feel this youth's perfections
          With an invisible and subtle stealth
          To creep in at mine eyes. Well, let it be.
          What ho, Malvolio!

                    Enter MALVOLIO

MALVOLIO   Here, madam, at your service.
OLIVIA Run after that same peevish messenger,   255
          The county's man. He left this ring behind him,
          Would I, or not. Tell him, I'll none of it.
          Desire him not to flatter with his lord,
          Nor hold him up with hopes; I am not for him.
          If that the youth will come this way tomorrow,   260
          I'll give him reasons for't. Hie thee, Malvolio!
MALVOLIO Madam, I will.   *Exit*
OLIVIA I do I know not what, and fear to find
          Mine eye too great a flatterer for my mind.
          Fate, show thy force; ourselves we do not owe.   265
          What is decreed must be; and be this so.   [*Exit*]

Looking back at Act 1
Activities for groups or individuals

1 Reality versus appearance

Act 1 reveals key aspects of the major characters: Orsino's self-indulgence, Viola's resourcefulness, the drunken Sir Toby's secret mocking of the foolish Sir Andrew, Feste's edgy humour, Malvolio's arrogance, and Olivia's readiness to abandon her mourning as she falls in love with Viola-Cesario. But all characters share something in common: they are affected in some way by the difference between reality and appearance. Write down the name of each character. Alongside each name write one or two sentences describing how they are affected by the difference between reality and appearance.

2 What is the play about? – other themes

Other themes of the play include music, love, the sea, disguise, folly. Write down two examples of each of these in Act 1.

3 Where is Illyria?

Historical Illyria lay along the Adriatic coast of present-day Albania and Croatia. But the Illyria of *Twelfth Night* is a never-never land of romantic comedy, where anything can happen. Imagine you are about to stage a production of the play. How will you present Illyria, the world of illusion? Will you give your production a Mediterranean atmosphere, a setting in Elizabethan England, or some other location? Look through the illustrations in this edition, then sketch and describe your own ideas for a set.

4 Five scenes, five headlines

There are five scenes in Act 1. Write five headlines to sum up the main action of each scene.

5 Viola-Cesario: young woman as young man

When Viola first appears as Cesario, do you think the audience should be able to recognise her immediately? Make notes on what she wears and other ways in which she tries to resemble a young man.

6 Determined by the stars?

At the end of Act 1, Olivia declares that 'Fate' will determine what happens to her love life. In Scene 3 Sir Toby says to Sir Andrew, 'Were we not born under Taurus?' as they enjoy their revels. Taurus (the bull) is one of the twelve signs of the zodiac. People who believe in astrology think that a person's character and personality are influenced by the star signs they are born under (you'll find that Act 2 begins with a character who says just that). But do *you* believe it? Make a list of reasons to explain why you agree or disagree with Sir Toby's belief.

7 Love at first sight? Echoes of Romeo

Love strikes like lightning in Act 1. Orsino fell in love with Olivia at first sight ('That instant was I turned into a hart'). Similarly, Viola has fallen in love with Orsino ('Whoe'er I woo, myself would be his wife'). Olivia asks herself 'Even so quickly may one catch the plague?' Romeo expresses similar amazement when he instantly falls in love on first seeing Juliet (*Romeo and Juliet*, Act 1 Scene 5, line 43).

Do you believe in love at first sight? Talk together about whether or not you believe you can fall head over heels in love 'in an instant'.

'O then unfold the passion of my love'. Compare this portrayal of Viola and Orsino with the pictures on pages vi, 56 and 159.

Antonio has rescued Sebastian from the shipwreck and wishes to be his servant. Sebastian rejects Antonio's offer and tells of his grief for his twin sister Viola, whom he believes drowned.

1 Parallel scenes (in pairs)

This scene has many echoes of Act 1 Scene 2. Take parts and read through the whole scene. Then go back and read Act 1 Scene 2. Identify the similarities by answering these questions:

- What kind of person rescued Viola and Sebastian?
- Where does each twin say they intend to go?
- Who wants to be the servant of each twin?
- What other parallels can you discover between Sebastian's situation and Viola's?
- If you were directing the play, would you have Sebastian dressed identically to Viola? And would you give him the same hairstyle, gestures and expressions? Give reasons for your decisions.

2 Antonio's feelings for Sebastian (in pairs)

At the end of this scene, Antonio decides to follow Sebastian to Orsino's court, even though he has many enemies there. Many productions of *Twelfth Night* use this scene to show that Antonio has a passionate affection for Sebastian, but is unwilling to show it openly. He offers to be Sebastian's servant, but Sebastian refuses the offer.

Take parts and read through the scene again, but this time the person who plays Antonio speaks his lines to Sebastian trying to hide his true feelings. However, in his soliloquy he fervently reveals how he genuinely feels. Afterwards talk together about whether you think this is how Antonio should be played on stage. Also discuss how you think Sebastian feels towards Antonio.

---

malignancy evil influence
distemper infect
sooth truly, indeed
determinate voyage plan for travel
mere extravagancy only wandering
in manners the rather in courtesy

breach surf, breaking waves
with such estimable wonder in all modesty
publish proclaim, describe
entertainment treatment, hospitality

Act 2 Scene 1
The sea-coast of Illyria

Enter ANTONIO and SEBASTIAN

ANTONIO Will you stay no longer? Nor will you not that I go with you?

SEBASTIAN By your patience, no. My stars shine darkly over me; the malignancy of my fate might perhaps distemper yours; therefore I shall crave of you your leave that I may bear my evils alone. It were a bad recompense for your love to lay any of them on you. 5

ANTONIO Let me know of you whither you are bound.

SEBASTIAN No, sooth, sir. My determinate voyage is mere extravagancy. But I perceive in you so excellent a touch of modesty that you will not extort from me what I am willing to keep in. Therefore it charges me in manners the rather to express myself. You must know 10 of me then, Antonio, my name is Sebastian (which I called Roderigo); my father was that Sebastian of Messaline whom I know you have heard of. He left behind him myself and a sister, both born in an hour: if the heavens had been pleased, would we had so ended! But you, sir, altered that, for some hour before you took 15 me from the breach of the sea was my sister drowned.

ANTONIO Alas the day!

SEBASTIAN A lady, sir, though it was said she much resembled me, was yet of many accounted beautiful; but though I could not with such estimable wonder overfar believe that, yet thus far I will boldly 20 publish her: she bore a mind that envy could not but call fair. She is drowned already, sir, with salt water, though I seem to drown her remembrance again with more.

ANTONIO Pardon me, sir, your bad entertainment.

SEBASTIAN O good Antonio, forgive me your trouble. 25

ANTONIO If you will not murder me for my love, let me be your servant.

Sebastian again rejects Antonio's offer of service, but Antonio determines to follow him in spite of all dangers. In Scene 2, Viola puzzles over Malvolio's message: has Olivia fallen in love with her?

1 'She took the ring of me' (in small groups)

Viola tells a downright lie to Malvolio in line 10. Why? Talk together about what it suggests to you about her character.

How does Malvolio return the ring? Invent a way for Malvolio to return the ring in a manner that suits his personality. In one production he disdainfully slipped it over his long staff and let it slide slowly down to Viola's feet. Speak 'Receive it so' and lines 11–13 as you explore various ideas.

---

recovered   saved from drowning
mine eyes will tell tales of me   I'll weep
on a moderate pace   without hurrying
desperate assurance   hopeless certainty

hardy   bold
peevishly   ill-temperedly
in starts distractedly   disjointedly and wildly

SEBASTIAN If you will not undo what you have done, that is, kill him whom you have recovered, desire it not. Fare ye well at once; my bosom is full of kindness, and I am yet so near the manners of my mother that, upon the least occasion more, mine eyes will tell tales 30 of me. I am bound to the Count Orsino's court. Farewell.   *Exit*

ANTONIO The gentleness of all the gods go with thee!
    I have many enemies in Orsino's court,
    Else would I very shortly see thee there.
    But come what may, I do adore thee so   35
    That danger shall seem sport, and I will go.   *Exit*

Act 2 Scene 2
A street near Olivia's house

Enter VIOLA and MALVOLIO

MALVOLIO Were you not even now with the Countess Olivia?

VIOLA Even now, sir; on a moderate pace, I have since arrived but hither.

MALVOLIO She returns this ring to you. You might have saved me my pains to have taken it away yourself. She adds, moreover, that you   5
should put your lord into a desperate assurance: she will none of him. And one thing more, that you be never so hardy to come again in his affairs, unless it be to report your lord's taking of this. Receive it so.

VIOLA She took the ring of me. I'll none of it.   10

MALVOLIO Come, sir, you peevishly threw it to her; and her will is, it should be so returned. If it be worth stooping for, there it lies, in your eye; if not, be it his that finds it.   *Exit*

VIOLA I left no ring with her: what means this lady?
    Fortune forbid my outside have not charmed her!   15
    She made good view of me, indeed so much
    That, methought, her eyes had lost her tongue,
    For she did speak in starts distractedly.

Perplexed, Viola fears Olivia loves her, whilst she herself loves Orsino. She hopes that time will resolve the difficulties. Scene 3 reveals that Sir Toby and Sir Andrew have been drinking all night.

1 Viola's soliloquy (activities for individuals or groups)

Viola realises (lines 14–38) that her disguise as a man has caused Olivia to fall in love with her. Appearance has triumphed over reality! Explore her soliloquy in one or more of the following ways:

a Learn the lines by heart and act them out as if you were auditioning for a place at drama school.

b The soliloquy is like a conversation. Viola asks herself questions and tries to answer them. In pairs, speak it as conversation. One partner reads a sentence (or short section that makes sense on its own). The other partner replies with the next small section.

c Walk around the room reading the lines aloud. At every new thought, change direction.

d Take parts as Viola, Olivia, Malvolio and Orsino. One person reads slowly. As any character is mentioned, everyone points at him or her: '"I" (*all point to Viola*) left no ring with "her" (*all point to Olivia*)', and so on. Who or what else is mentioned?

e Add gestures and facial expressions to illustrate each section.

2 Drunk again! (in pairs)

To establish a mood for Scene 3, take parts and read lines 1–12 in the style of drunken men. Say the lines very, very slowly as if you were befuddled, but trying to develop a logical argument.

---

churlish rude
pregnant enemy crafty fiend, the devil, Satan
proper-false handsome deceivers
waxen easily moulded, changeable
fadge turn out, develop
dote on be infatuated with
thriftless unprofitable, wasted

betimes early
diluculo surgere rising at dawn is healthy (a Latin saying)
by my troth truly
can tankard
four elements earth, air, fire and water

She loves me sure; the cunning of her passion
Invites me in this churlish messenger.   20
None of my lord's ring? Why, he sent her none;
I am the man; if it be so, as 'tis,
Poor lady, she were better love a dream.
Disguise, I see thou art a wickedness,
Wherein the pregnant enemy does much.   25
How easy is it for the proper-false
In women's waxen hearts to set their forms!
Alas, our frailty is the cause, not we,
For such as we are made of, such we be.
How will this fadge? My master loves her dearly,   30
And I (poor monster) fond as much on him
As she (mistaken) seems to dote on me.
What will become of this? As I am man,
My state is desperate for my master's love;
As I am woman – now alas the day! –   35
What thriftless sighs shall poor Olivia breathe?
O time, thou must untangle this, not I;
It is too hard a knot for me t'untie.   [*Exit*]

Act 2 Scene 3
A room in Olivia's house

Enter SIR TOBY and SIR ANDREW

SIR TOBY Approach, Sir Andrew. Not to be abed after midnight is to
   be up betimes, and *diluculo surgere*, thou know'st –
SIR ANDREW Nay, by my troth, I know not; but I know to be up late
   is to be up late.
SIR TOBY A false conclusion: I hate it as an unfilled can. To be up after   5
   midnight and to go bed then is early; so that to go to bed after
   midnight is to go to bed betimes. Does not our lives consist of the
   four elements?
SIR ANDREW Faith, so they say, but I think it rather consists of eating
   and drinking.   10

Feste mimics Sir Andrew's stupidity, and talks a good deal of nonsense. But Sir Andrew enjoys the joke and calls for a song. At Sir Toby's request, Feste sings a love song.

1 'We Three' – three fools (in groups of three)

In Shakespeare's time, a painting showing two asses (fools) was a popular inn sign. The spectator was the third fool! In some productions, Feste does some 'business' (actions) to illustrate 'We Three', for example sitting between the other two and pulling a face. Try one or both of the following:

a Design a modern version of the inn sign.

b Talk together about what other actions Feste might perform, then act out your version of the 'business' to show 'We Three'.

2 Taking the mickey out of Sir Andrew (in pairs)

Feste is mocking Sir Andrew without Sir Andrew realising it. 'Pigrogromitus', 'Vapians' and 'the equinoctial of Queubus' are all Shakespeare's nonsense inventions. Some critics have tried to make sense out of Feste's lines 23–5. Others think that they are nonsense, and Feste is simply laughing at Sir Andrew (and at learned people like critics!). Notice that Sir Toby had similarly mocked Sir Andrew's silliness at line 11, calling him 'a scholar'.

Talk together about whether you think lines 23–5 can make sense. Your guess is as good as anyone's! Note that 'I did impeticos thy gratillity' may have a kind of sense about it, as it could be Feste's way of saying 'thank you'.

3 Explore ways of delivering Feste's song (in small groups)

Experiment with different ways of singing (or speaking) Feste's song. It begins with hopes of love, but the second verse is poignantly bittersweet, saying seize the moment, because youth ends all too quickly.

---

stoup jug
catch song, round (where each singer 'catches' a tune or word after the previous singer)
breast voice
sooth truth

leman sweetheart
whipstock whip handle
Myrmidons soldiers of Achilles (a famous Greek warrior)
testril sixpence
still unsure always uncertain

SIR TOBY Th'art a scholar; let us therefore eat and drink. Marian, I say, a stoup of wine!

Enter CLOWN [FESTE]

SIR ANDREW Here comes the fool, i'faith.

FESTE How now, my hearts? Did you never see the picture of 'We Three'?   15

SIR TOBY Welcome, ass. Now let's have a catch.

SIR ANDREW By my troth, the fool has an excellent breast. I had rather than forty shillings I had such a leg, and so sweet a breath to sing, as the fool has. In sooth, thou wast in very gracious fooling last night, when thou spok'st of Pigrogromitus, of the Vapians passing   20
the equinoctial of Queubus. 'Twas very good, i'faith: I sent thee sixpence for thy leman; hadst it?

FESTE I did impeticos thy gratillity: for Malvolio's nose is no whipstock; my lady has a white hand, and the Myrmidons are no bottle-ale houses.   25

SIR ANDREW Excellent! Why this is the best fooling, when all is done. Now a song.

SIR TOBY Come on, there is sixpence for you. Let's have a song.

SIR ANDREW There's a testril of me, too; if one knight give a –

FESTE Would you have a love song or a song of good life?   30

SIR TOBY A love song, a love song.

SIR ANDREW Ay, ay. I care not for good life.

(Clown [Feste] sings)

> O mistress mine, where are you roaming?
> O stay and hear, your true love's coming,
>   That can sing both high and low.   35
> Trip no further, pretty sweeting;
> Journeys end in lovers meeting,
>   Every wise man's son doth know.

SIR ANDREW Excellent good, i'faith.

SIR TOBY Good, good.   40

FESTE [*Sings*]　　What is love? 'Tis not hereafter;
> Present mirth hath present laughter;
>   What's to come is still unsure.
> In delay there lies no plenty,
> Then come kiss me, sweet and twenty;   45
>   Youth's a stuff will not endure.

The three men sing together. Maria pleads with them to be quiet, but they carry on regardless. Malvolio enters and rebukes the revellers.

---

1 Making sense – and making noise! (in groups of five)

'Cataian', 'politicians' and 'Peg-a-Ramsey' might mean 'Chinese', 'schemers' and 'spoil-sport' respectively. Or they might just be nonsense inventions by Sir Toby. Take parts and enjoy this riotous scene – be loud and lively, and make lines 47–80 zing!

Malvolio's entrance invites every actor playing the part to astonish and amuse the audience (one Malvolio had curlers in his hair). Describe your image of Malvolio, called out of bed to stop the party.

---

mellifluous honey-like
contagious infectious, evil-smelling
 (Sir Toby implies that Feste has bad
 breath)
dulcet sweet
welkin sky
dog/dogs expert/mongrels (Feste
 puns: mongrels catch balls)

constrain'd ordered, commanded
caterwauling wailing like a cat
consanguineous related by blood
Beshrew me curse me
tinkers menders of pots and pans
coziers shoemakers
mitigation or remorse softening
Sneck up! Buzz off!

SIR ANDREW A mellifluous voice, as I am true knight.

SIR TOBY A contagious breath.

SIR ANDREW Very sweet, and contagious, i'faith.

SIR TOBY To hear by the nose, it is dulcet in contagion. But shall we   50
make the welkin dance indeed? Shall we rouse the night owl in a
catch that will draw three souls out of one weaver? Shall we do
that?

SIR ANDREW And you love me, let's do't: I am dog at a catch.

FESTE By'r lady, sir, and some dogs will catch well.   55

SIR ANDREW Most certain. Let our catch be, 'Thou knave'.

FESTE 'Hold thy peace, thou knave', knight? I shall be constrain'd in't
to call thee knave, knight.

SIR ANDREW 'Tis not the first time I have constrained one to call me
knave. Begin, fool. It begins, 'Hold thy peace.'   60

FESTE I shall never begin if I hold my peace.

SIR ANDREW Good, i'faith. Come, begin.

(*Catch sung*)

Enter MARIA

MARIA What a caterwauling do you keep here! If my lady have not
called up her steward Malvolio and bid him turn you out of doors,
never trust me.   65

SIR TOBY My lady's a Cataian, we are politicians, Malvolio's a
Peg-a-Ramsey, and [*Sings*] 'Three merry men be we.' Am not I
consanguineous? Am I not of her blood? Tilly vally! 'Lady!'
[*Sings*] 'There dwelt a man in Babylon, lady, lady.'

FESTE Beshrew me, the knight's in admirable fooling.   70

SIR ANDREW Ay, he does well enough if he be disposed, and so do I,
too; he does it with a better grace, but I do it more natural.

SIR TOBY [*Sings*] O'the twelfth day of December –

MARIA For the love o'God, peace!

Enter MALVOLIO

MALVOLIO My masters, are you mad? Or what are you? Have you no   75
wit, manners, nor honesty but to gabble like tinkers at this time
of night? Do ye make an alehouse of my lady's house, that ye squeak
out your coziers' catches without any mitigation or remorse of
voice? Is there no respect of place, persons, nor time in you?

SIR TOBY We did keep time, sir, in our catches. Sneck up!   80

Malvolio tells Sir Toby that Olivia wishes him to reform or leave her house. Sir Toby mocks Malvolio, who leaves, threatening Maria. She advises Sir Toby to behave, and begins to lay a plan to trick Malvolio.

1 Mocking Malvolio (in groups of four)

Sir Toby and Feste sing an old song to annoy Malvolio, refusing to take him seriously. Sir Toby forcefully reminds Malvolio of his inferior social status: 'Go, sir, rub your chain with crumbs' (as Olivia's steward, Malvolio wears a chain of office).

Take parts and act out the Malvolio episode in lines 75–105. Malvolio must try to remain dignified throughout, but Sir Toby should be as irritating as possible, with support from Feste. Maria must decide to what extent she will join in. Afterwards, talk together about whether or not you think Malvolio is being fairly treated. Is he just a killjoy, or has he good cause to rebuke Sir Toby?

2 'Cakes and ale' – feasting and drinking (in small groups)

In Shakespeare's time, puritans hated the church festivities and celebrations that went on at Christmas and Easter. Many puritans thought it was just an excuse to overeat and get drunk. 'Cakes and ale' is Sir Toby's metaphor for enjoyment and celebration (see p. 164). Equally offensive to puritans would have been Feste's mention of St Anne, mother of the Virgin Mary (line 100).

Either work out two tableaux (frozen pictures) to show, in turn, Sir Toby's and Malvolio's views of 'cakes and ale'.

Or write a poem to mock Malvolio entitled 'Cakes and ale'.

3 Malvolio's report to Olivia (in pairs)

Improvise Malvolio's report to Olivia on what has happened. Do it in character! Perhaps Olivia gently questions him.

---

round blunt
nothing allied to totally rejects
ginger spice for ale
give means . . . rule provide drinks for this disorderly party
the field to a duel

indignation angry challenge
gull trick
an ayword a famous fool
common recreation laughing-stock to everyone
puritan strait-laced killjoy

MALVOLIO Sir Toby, I must be round with you. My lady bade me tell you that, though she harbours you as her kinsman, she's nothing allied to your disorders. If you can separate yourself and your misdemeanours, you are welcome to the house; if not, and it would please you to take leave of her, she is very willing to bid you farewell. 85

SIR TOBY [*Sings*] Farewell, dear heart, since I must needs be gone.

MARIA Nay, good Sir Toby.

FESTE [*Sings*] His eyes do show his days are almost done.

MALVOLIO Is't even so?

SIR TOBY [*Sings*] But I will never die. 90

FESTE [*Sings*] Sir Toby, there you lie.

MALVOLIO This is much credit to you.

SIR TOBY [*Sings*] Shall I bid him go?

FESTE [*Sings*] What and if you do?

SIR TOBY [*Sings*] Shall I bid him go, and spare not? 95

FESTE [*Sings*] O no, no, no, no, you dare not.

SIR TOBY Out o'time, sir? Ye lie! Art any more than a steward? Dost thou think because thou art virtuous there shall be no more cakes and ale?

FESTE Yes, by St Anne, and ginger shall be hot i'th'mouth too. 100

[*Exit*]

SIR TOBY Th'art i'th'right. Go, sir, rub your chain with crumbs. A stoup of wine, Maria!

MALVOLIO Mistress Mary, if you prized my lady's favour at anything more than contempt, you would not give means for this uncivil rule; she shall know of it, by this hand. *Exit* 105

MARIA Go shake your ears.

SIR ANDREW 'Twere as good a deed as to drink when a man's a-hungry, to challenge him the field, and then to break promise with him, and make a fool of him.

SIR TOBY Do't, knight. I'll write thee a challenge, or I'll deliver thy indignation to him by word of mouth. 110

MARIA Sweet Sir Toby, be patient for tonight. Since the youth of the count's was today with my lady, she is much out of quiet. For Monsieur Malvolio, let me alone with him. If I do not gull him into an ayword, and make him a common recreation, do not think I have wit enough to lie straight in my bed. I know I can do it. 115

SIR TOBY Possess us, possess us, tell us something of him.

MARIA Marry, sir, sometimes he is a kind of puritan.

SIR ANDREW O if I thought that, I'd beat him like a dog! 120

Maria criticises Malvolio's self-importance and reveals her plan. She will write him a love letter, supposedly from Olivia. Malvolio's vanity will make a fool of him. Sir Toby again attempts to get more of Sir Andrew's money.

---

1 'Exquisite' – how does a drunk say that?

Exquisite is a very difficult word for a drunken man to say! Try speaking it as Sir Toby and Sir Andrew. Perhaps Sir Toby means 'exact'?

2 Planning to trick Malvolio (in groups of three)

Take parts as Maria, Sir Toby and Sir Andrew. Put your heads close together. Whisper lines 124–48 to each other, like conspirators plotting Malvolio's downfall. Afterwards, discuss how the lines could be delivered on stage to increase the audience's enjoyment.

3 Views of Malvolio – Maria's and Malvolio's (in pairs)

Maria lists how she sees Malvolio:

'a time-pleaser' – he's a time-server or sycophant (creep)
'an affectioned ass' – and an affected fool
'that cons state . . . swarths' – who learns high-sounding jargon
   by heart and quotes it endlessly
'The best persuaded of himself' – he thinks he's wonderful
'so crammed . . . excellencies' – and has every desirable quality
'that it is . . . love him' – he believes everyone loves him.

Take each description in turn and present two mimes for each:

- as Maria sees Malvolio
- as Malvolio sees himself.

4 'I was adored once, too' – a touching line?

Many directors use line 153 to make the audience feel sympathy towards Sir Andrew. How would you advise the actor to speak it?

---

epistles letters
gait walk
device trick
a horse of that colour just that
physic medicine, drug
Penthesilea queen of the Amazons (tall, fierce warrior-women)

beagle small hunting dog (Maria is small, unlike Penthesilea)
recover win (marry)
'cut' fool, horse without a tail, or female genitals
burn some sack warm up some wine

SIR TOBY What, for being a puritan? Thy exquisite reason, dear knight?

SIR ANDREW I have no exquisite reason for't, but I have reason good
enough.

MARIA The devil a puritan that he is, or anything constantly but a
time-pleaser, an affectioned ass, that cons state without book and   125
utters it by great swarths. The best persuaded of himself: so
crammed (as he thinks) with excellencies, that it is his grounds of
faith that all that look on him love him; and on that vice in him
will my revenge find notable cause to work.

SIR TOBY What wilt thou do?   130

MARIA I will drop in his way some obscure epistles of love, wherein
by the colour of his beard, the shape of his leg, the manner of his
gait, the expressure of his eye, forehead, and complexion, he shall
find himself most feelingly personated. I can write very like my lady
your niece; on a forgotten matter we can hardly make distinction   135
of our hands.

SIR TOBY Excellent, I smell a device.

SIR ANDREW I have't in my nose, too.

SIR TOBY He shall think by the letters that thou wilt drop that they
come from my niece, and that she's in love with him.   140

MARIA My purpose is indeed a horse of that colour.

SIR ANDREW And your horse now would make him an ass.

MARIA Ass, I doubt not.

SIR ANDREW O 'twill be admirable!

MARIA Sport royal, I warrant you: I know my physic will work with   145
him. I will plant you two, and let the fool make a third, where he
shall find the letter. Observe his construction of it. For this night,
to bed, and dream on the event. Farewell.   *Exit*

SIR TOBY Good night, Penthesilea.

SIR ANDREW Before me, she's a good wench.   150

SIR TOBY She's a beagle, true bred, and one that adores me. What
o'that?

SIR ANDREW I was adored once, too.

SIR TOBY Let's to bed, knight. Thou hadst need send for more money.

SIR ANDREW If I cannot recover your niece, I am a foul way out.   155

SIR TOBY Send for money, knight; if thou hast her not i'th'end, call
me 'cut'.

SIR ANDREW If I do not, never trust me; take it how you will.

SIR TOBY Come, come, I'll go burn some sack; 'tis too late to go to
bed now. Come, knight, come, knight.   160

Exeunt

Orsino calls for music to cheer him up, and sends for Feste. Orsino then claims that he is the model of all true lovers, because Olivia is constantly in his thoughts.

1 Mood music (in groups of five)

Lines 13–20 are very 'poetic'. Shakespeare gives them a musical background. Two of you speak the lines to each other. The other three provide an appropriate musical backing, such as humming gently, or quietly singing a love song. Experiment by changing parts. Find the version you like best.

2 Orsino – the example of 'all true lovers'? (in small groups)

As usual, Orsino is self-indulgently casting himself in the role of the 'true lover': melancholy, changeable, but obsessed with thoughts of his beloved. Has Orsino got it right, or is he just deceiving himself?

a Talk together about whether you agree that 'true lovers' always have a 'constant image' of their beloved in mind.

b What 'constant image' do you think Orsino really has in mind – Olivia? himself? some abstract notion of 'love'? or . . .?

c What is your definition of a 'true lover'?

3 Every picture tells a story

Theatre is a very powerful medium of communication, because spoken words are accompanied by physical images. Even actors who do not speak can convey a rich variety of meanings through the way in which they stand, move and relate to others on stage.

Viola does not speak until line 19. What is she doing up to then? Write a set of notes to help her to express her thoughts and feelings as Orsino speaks. Describe where she stands or sits (or lies) in relation to Orsino.

---

light airs   trivial tunes
recollected terms   artificial words
pangs   sufferings, pains
Unstaid and skittish   unstable and
  playful

all motions else   all other emotions
Save   except
constant image   unchanging
  vision
seat   (heart)

Act 2 Scene 4
Orsino's palace

Enter DUKE ORSINO, VIOLA, CURIO, and Lords and Musicians

ORSINO Give me some music –
                [*Musicians step forward*]
                     Now good morrow, friends;
    Now, good Cesario – but that piece of song,
    That old and antique song we heard last night;
    Methought it did relieve my passion much,
    More than light airs and recollected terms   5
    Of these most brisk and giddy-pacèd times.
    Come, but one verse.
CURIO He is not here, so please your lordship, that should sing it.
ORSINO Who was it?
CURIO Feste, the jester, my lord, a fool that the Lady Olivia's father   10
    took much delight in. He is about the house.
ORSINO Seek him out, and play the tune the while.
                           [*Exit Curio*]

              (*Music plays*)
    Come hither, boy; if ever thou shalt love,
    In the sweet pangs of it, remember me:
    For such as I am, all true lovers are,   15
    Unstaid and skittish in all motions else,
    Save in the constant image of the creature
    That is beloved. How dost thou like this tune?
VIOLA It gives a very echo to the seat
    Where love is throned.

Orsino advises Viola that women should marry men older than themselves, because men are fickle, and women soon lose their looks. He asks Feste to sing an old song of love.

1 Shakespeare's own experience? Your views?

Was Shakespeare thinking of his own marriage when he wrote lines 27–39? He married Anne Hathaway, who was eight years older than him. Orsino advises Viola that a woman should marry a man older than herself. She will thus be better able to keep her husband's affection, because men's emotions are more unstable than women's, and women's beauty quickly fades. Write a paragraph on each of the following, giving reasons for what you think of each:

- Shakespeare was thinking of his own experience in marriage.
- Orsino's advice is good advice.
- Men are more fickle than women.

2 More personal experience? (in pairs)

Orsino calls for a song. He uses an image that Shakespeare could have seen and heard in Stratford-upon-Avon: women outside their cottages spinning flax or wool, and young girls lace-making with bone bobbins, all singing at their work. Or perhaps he remembered what he saw as he walked from his lodgings in the City of London to the Globe on Bankside: the Huguenots, refugees from France, who became lacemakers and clothworkers.

a Read lines 41–6 aloud three or four times. Then close your eyes. Call up in your mind's eye the picture the lines evoke. Tell your partner what you 'see'.

b Discuss whether you think lines 41–6 are sincere, or just the dreamy fantasies of a self-indulgent, rich man, in love with the idea of being in love, and quite out of touch with reality.

---

stayed upon some favour   seen a face
i'faith?   Truly?
worn   frayed, worn out
hold the bent   stand the strain (like a bent longbow), stay constant

spinsters   women who spin flax or wool
free maids . . . bones   carefree girls who make lace with bone bobbins
silly sooth   simple truth
dallies   plays

ORSINO   Thou dost speak masterly.   20
    My life upon't, young though thou art, thine eye
    Hath stayed upon some favour that it loves;
    Hath it not, boy?
VIOLA   A little, by your favour.
ORSINO What kind of woman is't?
VIOLA   Of your complexion.
ORSINO She is not worth thee then. What years, i'faith?   25
VIOLA About your years, my lord.
ORSINO Too old, by heaven! Let still the woman take
    An elder than herself; so wears she to him;
    So sways she level in her husband's heart;
    For, boy, however we do praise ourselves,   30
    Our fancies are more giddy and unfirm,
    More longing, wavering, sooner lost and worn,
    Than women's are.
VIOLA   I think it well, my lord.
ORSINO Then let thy love be younger than thyself,
    Or thy affection cannot hold the bent: 35
    For women are as roses, whose fair flower,
    Being once displayed, doth fall that very hour.
VIOLA And so they are. Alas, that they are so:
    To die, even when they to perfection grow!

          Enter CURIO *and* CLOWN [FESTE]

ORSINO O fellow, come, the song we had last night.   40
    Mark it, Cesario, it is old and plain;
    The spinsters and the knitters in the sun,
    And the free maids that weave their thread with bones,
    Do use to chant it; it is silly sooth,
    And dallies with the innocence of love   45
    Like the old age.
FESTE Are you ready, sir?
ORSINO Ay, prithee sing.

Feste sings a sad song about a true lover who died for love. He leaves, commenting on Orsino's changeable moods. Orsino instructs Viola to tell Olivia that he loves not her wealth, but her beauty.

1 Feste's sorrowful song (in small groups)

Feste's song is about a melancholy lover who dies for love and wants to be forgotten. Cypress and yew trees were traditionally associated with death. They were, and still are, found in many churchyards. Coffins were often made of cypress wood ('sad cypress').

a Make up your own tune, or speak the song heavy-heartedly.

b Work out what everyone on stage does while Feste sings.

2 Is Feste mocking Orsino? (in pairs)

Talk together about whether you think Feste's song about a sad lover is mocking Orsino, who is also a melancholy lover. Decide if Feste is equally mocking Orsino in lines 70–4. To help your thinking, experiment with different ways of speaking the lines. Does Feste speak directly to Orsino, to members of the court, or to himself?

3 I love you, not your money (in pairs)

That's the message (lines 75–82) Orsino orders Viola to carry to Olivia, 'yond same sovereign cruelty'. To bring out Orsino's concern about choosing what he thinks are the right words to express his feelings, try the following. One person reads the lines aloud. The other echoes every high-flown phrase (e.g. 'sovereign cruelty', 'more noble than the world').

Afterwards, write the advice you would offer the actor. Suggest how, in speech and action, he could express Orsino's character through these eight lines.

Come away come hither
Fie away fly away
My part . . . share it I'm the truest lover who ever died for love
strown thrown (strewed)
melancholy god Saturn (whose planet was thought to rule melancholy people, see p. 35)

taffeta silk which changes colour
opal a jewel which seems to change colour
give place leave us
yond yonder
parts gifts
pranks adorns, beautifies

(*Music*)
The Song
Come away, come away, death,
And in sad cypress let me be laid. 50
Fie away, fie away, breath,
I am slain by a fair cruel maid;
　My shroud of white, stuck all with yew,
　　O prepare it.
My part of death no one so true 55
　Did share it.
Not a flower, not a flower sweet,
On my black coffin let there be strown;
Not a friend, not a friend greet
My poor corpse, where my bones shall be thrown: 60
　A thousand thousand sighs to save,
　　Lay me, O where
Sad true lover never find my grave,
　To weep there.

ORSINO There's for thy pains. [*Gives money*] 65
FESTE No pains, sir, I take pleasure in singing, sir.
ORSINO I'll pay thy pleasure then.
FESTE Truly, sir, and pleasure will be paid, one time or another.
ORSINO Give me now leave to leave thee.
FESTE Now the melancholy god protect thee, and the tailor make thy 70
　doublet of changeable taffeta, for thy mind is a very opal. I would
　have men of such constancy put to sea, that their business might
　be everything and their intent everywhere, for that's it that always
　makes a good voyage of nothing. Farewell. *Exit*
ORSINO Let all the rest give place.
　　　　　[*Curio and attendants retire*]
　　　　　　　　Once more, Cesario, 75
　Get thee to yond same sovereign cruelty.
　Tell her my love, more noble than the world,
　Prizes not quantity of dirty lands;
　The parts that fortune hath bestowed upon her
　Tell her I hold as giddily as fortune; 80
　But 'tis that miracle and queen of gems
　That nature pranks her in attracts my soul.
VIOLA But if she cannot love you, sir?
ORSINO I cannot be so answered.

Orsino claims that his capacity for love is greater than that of any woman.
Viola, hinting at her love for Orsino, says that women love as deeply as men,
and that men boast about being in love.

Viola's hints of her love for Orsino present every actor playing the duke with a
problem: how should he respond? Does he simply not notice, or does he begin
to suspect that his servant Cesario is not quite what 'he' seems? Is Orsino
unsettled by Viola's words? Discuss how you would advise Orsino to respond
as Viola speaks lines 101–18.

1 'Patience on a monument' (in small groups or individually)

Either devise a tableau (frozen picture) to represent lines 110–11.

Or write or draw what 'Patience on a monument, / Smiling at grief'
suggests to you. See page 165 for more on Viola's remarkable imagery.

Sooth in truth
pang of heart lovesickness
bide endure
motion of the liver passionate feeling
palate taste only
surfeit, cloyment, and revolt
 overeating, discomfort and being sick

damask pink
Our shows . . . will men claim more
than they feel
still always
denay denial

VIOLA	Sooth, but you must.	
	Say that some lady, as perhaps there is,	85
	Hath for your love as great a pang of heart	
	As you have for Olivia. You cannot love her.	
	You tell her so. Must she not then be answered?	

ORSINO There is no woman's sides
      Can bide the beating of so strong a passion   90
      As love doth give my heart; no woman's heart
      So big, to hold so much. They lack retention.
      Alas, their love may be called appetite,
      No motion of the liver, but the palate,
      That suffers surfeit, cloyment, and revolt,   95
      But mine is all as hungry as the sea,
      And can digest as much. Make no compare
      Between that love a woman can bear me,
      And that I owe Olivia.

VIOLA   Ay, but I know –

ORSINO What dost thou know?   100

VIOLA Too well what love women to men may owe.
      In faith, they are as true of heart as we.
      My father had a daughter loved a man
      As it might be perhaps, were I a woman,
      I should your lordship.

ORSINO   And what's her history?   105

VIOLA A blank, my lord. She never told her love,
      But let concealment like a worm i'th'bud
      Feed on her damask cheek. She pined in thought,
      And with a green and yellow melancholy
      She sat like Patience on a monument,   110
      Smiling at grief. Was not this love indeed?
      We men may say more, swear more, but indeed
      Our shows are more than will: for still we prove
      Much in our vows, but little in our love.

ORSINO But died thy sister of her love, my boy?   115

VIOLA I am all the daughters of my father's house,
      And all the brothers, too – and yet I know not.
      Sir, shall I to this lady?

ORSINO   Ay, that's the theme.
      To her in haste; give her this jewel; say
      My love can give no place, bide no denay.   120

Exeunt

Sir Toby and Fabian look forward to tricking Malvolio. Fabian has a personal grudge against Malvolio. Maria orders the men to hide and sets the trap for Malvolio: the forged letter.

---

1 The tricking of Malvolio (in groups of five)

Scene 5 makes delightfully funny theatre. It shows how Malvolio is 'gulled' (tricked) into making a fool of himself. To gain a first impression of how Malvolio's self-love and pomposity lead to his downfall, take parts as Sir Toby, Sir Andrew, Fabian, Maria and Malvolio. Read through the whole scene. Don't pause to discuss any words you don't understand – just go for it – enjoy yourselves!

2 Who is Fabian?

Malvolio has reported Fabian to Olivia for bear-baiting (a cruel 'sport' in which a bear, chained to a post, was attacked by dogs). So Fabian is in disgrace. But just who is he? A servant, or a gentleman hanger-on of some sort? Write a few paragraphs of Fabian's biography, telling who he is and how Malvolio caught him bear-baiting. Include what he looks like and how he's dressed. Use the tiny clue that he has organised a bear-baiting at Olivia's – what kind of man would do that?

3 Imagery (in pairs)

Lines 1–19 contain vivid imagery (see pp. 164–5). Talk together about the meaning of each of the following. Which one is still in use?

Lines 2–3 'boiled to death with melancholy'

Line 5 'sheep-biter' (an insult, meaning 'woman-chaser' or 'puritan')

Lines 8–9 'fool him black and blue'

Line 12 'metal of India' (Sir Toby uses other fantastic terms to describe Maria. What does it suggest about their relationship?)

Line 16 'contemplative idiot' (Show your partner what this looks like!)

Lines 18–19 'the trout that must be caught by tickling' – flattery (trout can be caught by gently stroking them to lull them into a false sense of security).

---

scruple tiny part
niggardly stingy, mean
exult rejoice

box-tree evergreen
shrub
Close hide

Act 2 Scene 5
Olivia's garden

Enter SIR TOBY, SIR ANDREW and FABIAN

SIR TOBY Come thy ways, Signior Fabian.

FABIAN Nay, I'll come. If I lose a scruple of this sport, let me be boiled
to death with melancholy.

SIR TOBY Wouldst thou not be glad to have the niggardly rascally
sheep-biter come by some notable shame?   5

FABIAN I would exult, man. You know he brought me out o'favour with
my lady about a bear-baiting here.

SIR TOBY To anger him, we'll have the bear again; and we will fool
him black and blue, shall we not, Sir Andrew?

SIR ANDREW And we do not, it is pity of our lives.   10

SIR TOBY Here comes the little villain.

Enter MARIA

How now, my metal of India?

MARIA Get ye all three into the box-tree. Malvolio's coming down this
walk. He has been yonder i'the sun practising behaviour to his own
shadow this half hour. Observe him, for the love of mockery, for   15
I know this letter will make a contemplative idiot of him. Close,
in the name of jesting!

[*The men hide*]

Lie thou there [*Drops a letter*]; for here comes the trout that must
be caught with tickling.   *Exit*

Malvolio reveals his private fantasies. He daydreams aloud, persuading himself that Olivia loves him, and imagining that they are married. Sir Toby and Sir Andrew are enraged.

1 Overhearing: how do they hide? (in small groups)

Every director of the play seizes the challenge of 'the box-tree' (literally, an evergreen shrub), and aims to make this overhearing scene as hilarious as possible. There's a huge amount of potential laughter in how Sir Toby and his friends hide. They are always on the brink of being seen by Malvolio, but just manage to avoid discovery. In different productions they have hidden behind benches, trees, hedges, statues, walls and windows. Sometimes they have even posed as garden statues!

Work out how to stage their 'hiding' to greatest comic effect.

2 Malvolio's day-dreaming – and a near slip! (in pairs)

Malvolio fantasises about becoming a count and enjoying sex with Olivia. He relishes the thought of disdainfully condescending to Sir Toby. But he almost slips at lines 50–1: what was he thinking of playing with before he changed his thought to 'some rich jewel'?

3 'The Lady of the Strachy' – invent her story

Nobody knows just who Shakespeare had in mind when Malvolio mentions the lady who married beneath her ('the yeoman of the wardrobe' is a servant). Write the story of what happened.

4 Ways of looking haughtily at inferiors

Try imitating two of Malvolio's ways of looking superior:
Lines 44–5 'demure travel of regard' (a cool look at the servants)
Line 55 'austere regard of control' (a cold and superior stare).

---

fortune   luck, destiny
affect   admire
fancy   love
overweening   immensely
  conceited
jets   struts

advanced plumes   puffed-out feathers
  (like a turkey-cock)
'Slight   by God's light (an oath)
Jezebel   shameless woman
stone-bow   catapult
branched   embroidered

Enter MALVOLIO

MALVOLIO 'Tis but fortune; all is fortune. Maria once told me she did   20
affect me, and I have heard herself come thus near, that should she
fancy, it should be one of my complexion. Besides, she uses me with
a more exalted respect than any one else that follows her. What
should I think on't?

SIR TOBY Here's an overweening rogue!   25

FABIAN O peace! Contemplation makes a rare turkey-cock of him; how
he jets under his advanced plumes!

SIR ANDREW 'Slight, I could so beat the rogue!

FABIAN Peace, I say!

MALVOLIO To be Count Malvolio!   30

SIR TOBY Ah, rogue!

SIR ANDREW Pistol him, pistol him!

FABIAN Peace, peace!

MALVOLIO There is example for't: the Lady of the Strachy married
the yeoman of the wardrobe –   35

SIR ANDREW Fie on him, Jezebel!

FABIAN O peace! Now he's deeply in. Look how imagination blows him.

MALVOLIO Having been three months married to her, sitting in my state –

SIR TOBY O for a stone-bow to hit him in the eye!

MALVOLIO Calling my officers about me, in my branched velvet gown,   40
having come from a day-bed, where I have left Olivia sleeping –

SIR TOBY Fire and brimstone!

FABIAN O peace, peace!

MALVOLIO And then to have the humour of state; and after a demure
travel of regard – telling them I know my place, as I would they   45
should do theirs – to ask for my kinsman Toby –

SIR TOBY Bolts and shackles!

FABIAN O peace, peace, peace! Now, now.

MALVOLIO Seven of my people, with an obedient start, make out for
him. I frown the while, and perchance wind up my watch, or play   50
with my – some rich jewel. Toby approaches; curtsies there to me –

SIR TOBY Shall this fellow live?

FABIAN Though our silence be drawn from us by th'ears, yet peace!

MALVOLIO I extend my hand to him thus, quenching my familiar smile
with an austere regard of control –   55

SIR TOBY And does not 'Toby' take you a blow o'the lips then?

Fabian tries to prevent Sir Toby's enraged comments being overheard. Malvolio discovers the letter and thinks that he recognises the handwriting as Olivia's. He tries to figure out the contents.

Which line opposite do you think best fits this moment? Prepare your own version of Malvolio's letter-reading. Give him plenty of time to puzzle out the meaning – it makes the scene even funnier.

1 Very rude!

Shakespeare put a crude joke into lines 72–5. Elizabethans knew that 'cut' was slang for the female genitals, and they would hear 'P's' as 'pees'. They would probably find it very funny that Sir Andrew fails to see the dirty joke. In modern productions, directors have to decide what to do with the lines. What would you do? For example, is Malvolio fully aware of what he is saying?

2 'What employment have we here?'

Malvolio's discovery of the letter can be hilarious (in one production it stuck to his shoe). How would you stage the 'discovery'?

---

prerogative right
sinews strength
woodcock near the gin bird near the trap
the spirit . . . intimate the god of emotions suggests
in contempt of without
impressure stamp

Lucrece seal-ring (representing Lucrece, the model of chastity)
liver source of passion
Jove king of the gods (see p. 165)
numbers verses, metre
brock badger
gore wound, make bloody
fustian bombastic, pretentious

MALVOLIO Saying, 'Cousin Toby, my fortunes having cast me on your
    niece, give me this prerogative of speech – '
SIR TOBY What, what?
MALVOLIO 'You must amend your drunkenness.'   60
SIR TOBY Out, scab!
FABIAN Nay, patience, or we break the sinews of our plot.
MALVOLIO 'Besides, you waste the treasure of your time with a foolish
    knight – '
SIR ANDREW That's me, I warrant you.   65
MALVOLIO 'One Sir Andrew – '
SIR ANDREW I knew 'twas I, for many do call me fool.
MALVOLIO [*Taking up the letter*] What employment have we here?
SIR TOBY Now is the woodcock near the gin.
FABIAN O peace, and the spirit of humours intimate reading aloud to   70
    him!
MALVOLIO By my life, this is my lady's hand: these be her very c's,
    her u's, and her t's, and thus makes she her great P's. It is, in
    contempt of question, her hand.
SIR ANDREW Her c's, her u's, and her t's: why that?   75
MALVOLIO [*Reads*] 'To the unknown beloved, this, and my good
    wishes' – her very phrases! By your leave, wax. Soft! And the
    impressure her Lucrece, with which she uses to seal: 'tis my lady.
    To whom should this be? [*Opens the letter*]
FABIAN This wins him, liver and all.   80
MALVOLIO [*Reads*]   Jove knows I love,
                           But who?
                      Lips, do not move:
                      No man must know.
    'No man must know.' What follows? The numbers altered! 'No   85
    man must know'! If this should be thee, Malvolio!
SIR TOBY Marry, hang thee, brock!
MALVOLIO [*Reads*]   I may command where I adore,
                      But silence, like a Lucrece knife,
                      With bloodless stroke my heart doth gore;   90
                      M.O.A.I. doth sway my life.
FABIAN A fustian riddle!
SIR TOBY Excellent wench, say I.
MALVOLIO 'M.O.A.I. doth sway my life.' Nay, but first let me see, let
    me see, let me see.   95

Malvolio persuades himself that Olivia has written the poem to him. He reads what follows: that he should transform himself from a steward into a great gentleman – and wear yellow stockings and cross-garters!

1 Reading the letter (in small groups)

Lines 118–32 give every actor playing Malvolio a great chance to entertain the audience. Most read the letter slowly, sentence by sentence. They leave long pauses in which they can insert much stage business (actions, gestures), milking the speech for laughs. For example, at 'revolve' (line 119), one Malvolio slowly turned round and round with increasing glee, as if he had made a great discovery.

a Work on the letter a sentence at a time. For each sentence or phrase, create stage business that you think will entertain the audience.

b What do the overhearers do as Malvolio reads? They'll certainly be finding it hard to stop laughing. But imagine that they put on a little show for each other to illustrate each sentence of the letter, and mock Malvolio at the same time. Perform their parody that takes place behind Malvolio's back.

2 Hawking and hunting – Elizabethan England

Sir Toby and Fabian use images from Elizabethan field sports as they comment on Malvolio's puzzlement:

'with what wing the staniel checks at it' – how quickly the kestrel flies mistakenly at it
'cold scent' – the hounds have lost the fox
'Sowter will cry' – the hound (named Sowter) will bark
'excellent at faults' – can find the fox when the scent is lost.

You can find more on echoes of Elizabethan England on page 170.

dressed prepared
formal capacity normal
 intelligence
rank smelly
no consonancy . . . probation no
 consistency that stands up to test
detraction disasters
simulation appearance

inure accustom
cast thy humble slough get rid of
 your humble manner (like a snake
 casting off its old skin)
tang . . . state speak loudly about
 politics
the trick of singularity distinctive
 behaviour and dress

FABIAN What dish o'poison has she dressed him!

SIR TOBY And with what wing the staniel checks at it!

MALVOLIO 'I may command where I adore.' Why, she may command me: I serve her; she is my lady. Why, this is evident to any formal capacity. There is no obstruction in this, and the end – what should   100
that alphabetical position portend? If I could make that resemble something in me – Softly! 'M.O.A.I.' –

SIR TOBY O ay, make up that! He is now at a cold scent.

FABIAN Sowter will cry upon't for all this, though it be as rank as a fox.   105

MALVOLIO 'M' – Malvolio. 'M' – why, that begins my name!

FABIAN Did not I say he would work it out? The cur is excellent at faults.

MALVOLIO 'M' – but then there is no consonancy in the sequel that suffers under probation. 'A' should follow, but 'O' does.   110

FABIAN And O shall end, I hope.

SIR TOBY Ay, or I'll cudgel him and make him cry 'O'!

MALVOLIO And then 'I' comes behind.

FABIAN Ay, and you had any eye behind you, you might see more detraction at your heels than fortunes before you.   115

MALVOLIO 'M.O.A.I.' This simulation is not as the former, and yet, to crush this a little, it would bow to me, for every one of these letters are in my name. Soft, here follows prose. [*Reads*] 'If this fall into thy hand, revolve. In my stars I am above thee, but be not afraid of greatness. Some are born great, some achieve greatness,   120
and some have greatness thrust upon 'em. Thy fates open their hands; let thy blood and spirit embrace them, and, to inure thyself to what thou art like to be, cast thy humble slough and appear fresh. Be opposite with a kinsman, surly with servants; let thy tongue tang arguments of state; put thyself into the trick of singularity. She thus   125
advises thee that sighs for thee. Remember who commended thy yellow stockings and wished to see thee ever cross-gartered: I say, remember. Go to, thou art made if thou desir'st to be so; if not, let me see thee a steward still, the fellow of servants, and not worthy to touch Fortune's fingers. Farewell. She that would alter services   130
with thee,

The Fortunate-Unhappy.'

Malvolio is overjoyed. He is supremely confident that Olivia loves him. He will follow the instructions in every detail – even smiling! The conspirators are ecstatic about the success of their plot.

1 Malvolio is caught! Show his delight (in pairs)

Malvolio's joy knows no bounds. The trick has worked, and Malvolio is caught in the net of his own self-importance. Explore ways of speaking lines 133–47 to find the most entertaining presentation. Here are some suggestions to help you work out a final version:

- One person reads. The other echoes every 'I', 'me', 'my'.
- Echo and emphasise every verb: 'discovers', 'is', 'will', etc.
- Create a gesture or action for every sentence or phrase.
- Read the postscript (lines 143–6) in different ways (e.g. very fast, with increasing delight, or with puzzlement).
- Turn the lines into a conversation. Each partner reads alternate sentences or phrases. Try to outdo each other in joyfulness!
- One partner reads each sentence (or phrase) as a question. The other repeats it immediately as an emphatic statement. At 'I will smile', use all kinds of ways of showing Malvolio's difficulty in producing a smile!
- '*Exit*'. How does Malvolio leave the stage? Practise different ways in which he might go off. Decide the style you most prefer to give the audience maximum enjoyment.

2 Sir Andrew – a repetitive ninny (in pairs)

Sir Andrew has no thoughts of his own. Read aloud everything he says in the script opposite. Also say the line immediately before each of Sir Andrew's sentences. Use a tone of voice to bring out his empty-headedness.

---

champain   open country
baffle   humiliate
point-device   in every detail
jade   deceive, trick
injunction   order
habits   clothes
strange, stout   aloof, proud

Jove   king of the gods (see p. 165)
sophy   shah of Persia (see p. 100)
dowry   marriage gift
tray-trip   a dice game (won by throwing a three)
acqua-vitae   brandy
Tartar   hell

Daylight and champain discovers not more! This is open. I will be proud, I will read politic authors, I will baffle Sir Toby, I will wash off gross acquaintance, I will be point-device, the very man. I do not now fool myself to let imagination jade me; for every reason excites to this, that my lady loves me. She did commend my yellow stockings of late, she did praise my leg being cross-gartered; and in this she manifests herself to my love, and with a kind of injunction drives me to these habits of her liking. I thank my stars, I am happy. I will be strange, stout, in yellow stockings, and cross-gartered, even with the swiftness of putting on. Jove and my stars be praised! Here is yet a postscript. [*Reads*] 'Thou canst not choose but know who I am. If thou entertain'st my love, let it appear in thy smiling; thy smiles become thee well. Therefore in my presence still smile, dear my sweet, I prithee.' Jove, I thank thee. I will smile; I will do every thing that thou wilt have me.   *Exit*

FABIAN I will not give my part of this sport for a pension of thousands to be paid from the sophy.

SIR TOBY I could marry this wench for this device –

SIR ANDREW So could I, too.

SIR TOBY And ask no other dowry with her but such another jest.

SIR ANDREW Nor I neither.

FABIAN Here comes my noble gull-catcher.

Enter MARIA

SIR TOBY Wilt thou set thy foot o'my neck?

SIR ANDREW Or o'mine either?

SIR TOBY Shall I play my freedom at tray-trip and become thy bondslave?

SIR ANDREW I'faith, or I either?

SIR TOBY Why, thou hast put him in such a dream that when the image of it leaves him, he must run mad.

MARIA Nay, but say true, does it work upon him?

SIR TOBY Like acqua-vitae with a midwife.

MARIA If you will then see the fruits of the sport, mark his first approach before my lady. He will come to her in yellow stockings, and 'tis a colour she abhors, and cross-gartered, a fashion she detests; and he will smile upon her, which will now be so unsuitable to her disposition, being addicted to a melancholy as she is, that it cannot but turn him into a notable contempt. If you will see it, follow me.

SIR TOBY To the gates of Tartar, thou most excellent devil of wit!

SIR ANDREW I'll make one, too.   *Exeunt*

Looking back at Act 2
Activities for groups or individuals

1 Five locations, common themes, vivid images

a **Settings**   The five scenes of Act 2 are set on the sea-coast, in a street outside Olivia's house, inside Olivia's house, at Duke Orsino's and in Olivia's garden. Design a set to show how you would ensure that the action on stage flows smoothly from scene to scene, without interruption or long delays for scene-shifting.

b **Themes**   The locations may change, but each scene contains common themes: love, and appearance versus reality. For each scene write how the theme of love occurs (who loves whom), and how someone is deceived because appearance does not match reality. In Scene 1 the two themes are simply expressed: Antonio loves Sebastian, and there is only minor 'deception' (Sebastian calls himself Roderigo, and believes that Viola is drowned). But both themes run through Scenes 2, 3, 4 and 5 in more complex ways.

c **Imagery**   Every scene includes striking imagery (see pp. 164–5). Find a way of presenting the following images (e.g. in a tableau or drawing), then choose an image of your own from each scene and express them in a way you feel appropriate.
   Scene 1   'My stars shine darkly over me' (line 2)
   Scene 2   'Disguise, I see thou art a wickedness' (line 24)
   Scene 3   'cakes and ale' (lines 98–9)
   Scene 4   'Now the melancholy god protect thee' (line 70)
   Scene 5   'here comes the trout that must be caught with tickling' (lines 18–19)

2 Maria: 'My niece's chambermaid'

Sir Toby describes Maria as 'little villain' and 'metal of India'. He jokes twice about her height, calling her first 'Penthesilea' (queen of the Amazons, a race of tall, fierce warrior-women) and then 'beagle' (a small hunting dog). Viola pleads 'Some mollification for your giant, sweet lady' as Maria tries to persuade her to leave Olivia's house.

Talk together about whether it would increase the audience's amusement to cast a tall or a short actor as Maria. Consider who could play Maria (people you have seen in films or on television or stage, or your friends!) – and why.

3 Different viewpoints on romantic love

To gain a quite different view of the discussion of love between Orsino and Viola, try this activity, working in groups of four. Two of you are Orsino and Viola. The other two are palace cleaners, on your hands and knees scrubbing the floor. Orsino and Viola read lines 75–121 from Scene 4, pausing frequently. They are totally oblivious of the cleaners, who are scrubbing away near their feet. The cleaners hear everything, and comment loudly to each other on all that's said. They have a much more down-to-earth and cynical view of love!

Fabian, Sir Toby and Sir Andrew watch Malvolio swallow the bait. In some productions, they crawl frantically around the stage to avoid discovery as Malvolio strolls about, totally self-obsessed. In one production, Sir Andrew became a garden bench and Malvolio sat on him!

Decide where you could stage the gulling scene in the open air somewhere around your school or college. One college production had the conspirators dodging among dustbins – and sometimes jumping into them.

4 Feste's songs – express their poignant mood

In Scene 3 Feste's song ends with a reminder that 'Youth's a stuff will not endure'. In Scene 4 his melancholy song tells of the lover who dies because he is rejected by 'a fair cruel maid'. Experiment with ways of presenting both songs, singing or speaking them.

Feste juggles with words, declining to give Viola a straight answer. He comments sceptically on the slipperiness of language, on Viola herself, and on the foolishness of husbands.

1 Feste: 'her corrupter of words' (in pairs)

Feste's joking and punning arises from the slipperiness of language: 'words are very rascals' (line 17) and 'words are grown so false' (lines 20–1). Feste enjoys playing with different meanings of the same word (for example 'live' = 'earn money' or 'have a house'). Yet he jokingly accuses Viola of doing just the same – twisting words to give them different meanings ('A sentence is but a cheveril glove to a good wit', lines 9–10).

When Feste says that words have become unreliable 'since bonds [promises] disgraced them', he is probably pointing once again to the way in which a word can change its meaning. Promises are made of words, but because words can be interpreted differently, it's difficult to keep promises.

To gain a sense of how Feste keeps twisting Viola's questions and statements, take parts and speak lines 1–49. Afterwards, use the information on this page and on page 72 to help you understand words or phrases you may not know.

Save thee may God preserve you (traditional greeting)

tabor small side-drum

cheveril soft leather

dally nicely play cleverly

wanton loose, disreputable, unchaste

bonds promises

loath to prove reason reluctant to argue logically

Act 3 Scene 1
In Olivia's orchard

Enter VIOLA *and* FESTE, *playing on a pipe and tabor*

VIOLA Save thee, friend, and thy music! Dost thou live by thy tabor?

FESTE No, sir, I live by the church.

VIOLA Art thou a churchman?

FESTE No such matter, sir. I do live by the church; for I do live at my house, and my house doth stand by the church. 5

VIOLA So thou mayst say the king lies by a beggar, if a beggar dwell near him; or the church stands by thy tabor if thy tabor stand by the church.

FESTE You have said, sir. To see this age! A sentence is but a cheveril glove to a good wit – how quickly the wrong side may be turned 10 outward!

VIOLA Nay, that's certain: they that dally nicely with words may quickly make them wanton.

FESTE I would therefore my sister had had no name, sir.

VIOLA Why, man? 15

FESTE Why, sir, her name's a word, and to dally with that word might make my sister wanton; but, indeed, words are very rascals, since bonds disgraced them.

VIOLA Thy reason, man?

FESTE Truth, sir, I can yield you none without words, and words are 20 grown so false, I am loath to prove reason with them.

VIOLA I warrant thou art a merry fellow and car'st for nothing.

FESTE Not so, sir, I do care for something; but in my conscience, sir, I do not care for you: if that be to care for nothing, I would it would make you invisible. 25

VIOLA Art not thou the Lady Olivia's fool?

FESTE No, indeed, sir. The Lady Olivia has no folly. She will keep no fool, sir, till she be married, and fools are as like husbands as pilchards are to herrings – the husband's the bigger. I am indeed not her fool but her corrupter of words. 30

Feste, still juggling with words, talks Viola into giving him money. She reflects on the need for fools to be clever. Sir Toby invites Viola to visit Olivia.

1 Shakespeare: playwright of his times (in pairs)

Shakespeare's plays often contain references to the theatre and to other matters familiar to his Elizabethan audiences:

Pandarus, Cressida, Troilus (lines 43–4) Shakespeare's *Troilus and Cressida* is a play about two young lovers, set during the siege of Troy by the Greeks. Pandarus was the Trojan lord who acted as go-between for the ill-starred young lovers.

'I might say "element"' (line 49) Shakespeare may be defending a fellow playwright, Ben Jonson, who was attacked for his fondness for using the word 'element'. Talk together about what someone means when they say 'It's out of my element'. Also discuss whether, in the previous line, Feste sees through Viola's disguise.

A tribute to an actor? Lines 50–8 may be Shakespeare's tribute to Robert Armin, the actor who first played Feste. Talk together about the general sense of the lines, namely that the really good joker ('wise fool') suits his humour to the particular audience and occasion, rather than cracking jokes about everything. It will help your discussion to use modern comedians as examples.

Speaking French Lines 61–2 mean 'God save you, sir' / 'And you also; your servant'. Why might Sir Andrew speak French?

Dramatic irony A powerful technique much used by Shakespeare (see p. 156). Viola's Aside (line 40) is a great opportunity to make the audience laugh or smile. Advise the actor how to speak it.

---

late recently	**craves** demands
orb Earth	**haggard** wild, untamed hawk
your wisdom 'your worship'	**check** fly at
and thou pass upon if you joke about	**fit** appropriate
	folly-fall'n behaving foolishly
conster explain (construe)	**Save you** God save you
out of my welkin unknown to me	**list** objective, purpose

VIOLA   I saw thee late at the Count Orsino's.

FESTE   Foolery, sir, does walk about the orb like the sun; it shines
everywhere. I would be sorry, sir, but the fool should be as oft
with your master as with my mistress: I think I saw your wisdom
there.   35

VIOLA   Nay, and thou pass upon me, I'll no more with thee. Hold,
there's expenses for thee. [*Gives a coin*]

FESTE   Now Jove, in his next commodity of hair, send thee a beard!

VIOLA   By my troth, I'll tell thee, I am almost sick for one – [*Aside*]
though I would not have it grow on my chin. Is thy lady within?   40

FESTE   Would not a pair of these have bred, sir?

VIOLA   Yes, being kept together and put to use.

FESTE   I would play Lord Pandarus of Phrygia, sir, to bring a Cressida
to this Troilus.

VIOLA   I understand you sir; 'tis well begged. [*Gives another coin*]   45

FESTE   The matter, I hope, is not great, sir – begging but a beggar:
Cressida was a beggar. My lady is within, sir. I will conster to them
whence you come. Who you are, and what you would are out of
my welkin – I might say 'element', but the word is overworn.

Exit

VIOLA   This fellow is wise enough to play the fool,   50
And to do that well craves a kind of wit;
He must observe their mood on whom he jests,
The quality of persons, and the time;
Not, like the haggard, check at every feather
That comes before his eye. This is a practice,   55
As full of labour as a wise man's art:
For folly that he wisely shows is fit;
But wise men, folly-fall'n, quite taint their wit.

Enter SIR TOBY *and* [SIR] ANDREW

SIR TOBY   Save you, gentleman.

VIOLA   And you, sir.   60

SIR ANDREW   *Dieu vous garde, monsieur.*

VIOLA   *Et vous aussi; votre serviteur.*

SIR ANDREW   I hope, sir, you are, and I am yours.

SIR TOBY   Will you encounter the house? My niece is desirous you
should enter, if your trade be to her.   65

VIOLA   I am bound to your niece, sir; I mean, she is the list of my voyage.

Viola-Cesario gives punning replies to Sir Toby. Sir Andrew is impressed by Viola-Cesario's elegant language, and determines to copy it. Olivia begins to reveal her true feelings to Viola-Cesario.

1 Punning is infectious (in pairs)

Viola has just experienced Feste's playfulness with language. Now she is quick to make similar puns in answer to Sir Toby's mocking. One person reads lines 68–9 and 71. The other makes appropriate gestures to highlight the puns on 'understand' and 'gait' (step, or gate).

2 Sir Andrew's responses

Viola addresses Olivia in highly elaborate, courteous speech. Her compliments greatly impress Sir Andrew. Advise the actor playing Sir Andrew how he should behave at each of the following moments:

- As he says 'well' (line 73), is he impressed? contemptuous?
- 'I'll get 'em all three' (lines 76–7): is he memorising the words, or writing them down in a notebook? Or . . .?
- When Olivia says 'leave me' (line 78), how does Sir Andrew exit with Maria and Sir Toby? Willingly? Reluctant to go? Or . . .? (Remember he's only visiting Sir Toby in order to woo Olivia, and he's probably not had a chance even to talk with her.)

3 'Music from the spheres'

Many Elizabethans believed that the planets were contained in concentric crystal spheres. The spheres rotated, creating wonderfully harmonious music that could not be heard by humans. If Shakespeare were writing today, what modern comparison might he substitute for line 95, 'music from the spheres', to describe the most wonderful music?

Taste try out	**blanks** blank sheets of paper
gait step (or gate)	**whet** sharpen, tempt
odours perfume	**suit** cause
pregnant ready	**solicit** plead for, entreat
vouchsafed willing	**enchantment** bewitchment (causing
lowly feigning pretended humility	Olivia to love Viola-Cesario)

SIR TOBY Taste your legs, sir; put them to motion.

VIOLA My legs do better understand me, sir, than I understand what
you mean by bidding me taste my legs.

SIR TOBY I mean, to go, sir, to enter.   70

VIOLA I will answer you with gait and entrance – but we are prevented.

Enter OLIVIA *and* GENTLEWOMAN [MARIA]

Most excellent accomplished lady, the heavens rain odours on you!

SIR ANDREW That youth's a rare courtier – 'rain odours' – well.

VIOLA My matter hath no voice, lady, but to your own most pregnant
and vouchsafed ear.   75

SIR ANDREW 'Odours', 'pregnant', and 'vouchsafed': I'll get 'em all
three all ready.

OLIVIA Let the garden door be shut, and leave me to my hearing.
                    [*Exeunt Sir Toby, Sir Andrew, and Maria*]
Give me your hand, sir.

VIOLA My duty, madam, and most humble service.   80

OLIVIA What is your name?

VIOLA Cesario is your servant's name, fair princess.

OLIVIA My servant, sir? 'Twas never merry world
　　　　Since lowly feigning was called compliment.
　　　　Y'are servant to the Count Orsino, youth.   85

VIOLA And he is yours, and his must needs be yours:
　　　　Your servant's servant is your servant, madam.

OLIVIA For him, I think not on him; for his thoughts,
　　　　Would they were blanks, rather than filled with me!

VIOLA Madam, I come to whet your gentle thoughts   90
　　　　On his behalf.

OLIVIA　　　　　　　　O by your leave, I pray you!
　　　　I bade you never speak again of him;
　　　　But would you undertake another suit
　　　　I had rather hear you to solicit that,
　　　　Than music from the spheres.

VIOLA　　　　　　　　　　　　　　Dear lady –   95

OLIVIA Give me leave, beseech you. I did send,
　　　　After the last enchantment you did here,
　　　　A ring in chase of you. So did I abuse
　　　　Myself, my servant, and, I fear me, you.

Olivia hints at the agonies of love she feels. She says her feelings are clearly visible. After seeming to dismiss Viola-Cesario, Olivia calls her back. Viola-Cesario declares that she is not what she seems.

1 Love and cruelty – fierce animal comparisons

a **Bear-baiting** (see p. 58) In lines 103–5, Olivia uses the image of bear-baiting ('stake', 'baited' and 'unmuzzled') to describe how her secret love for Viola-Cesario tears at her. The image conjures up a picture of Olivia chained and baited like a bear by the 'unmuzzled thoughts' of Viola-Cesario's cruel heart.

b **Lions and wolves** Who does Olivia have in mind in line 114? Does she think of Viola-Cesario as the lion (proud creature) or the wolf (cruel predator)? Or might she be thinking of Orsino as the lion? Talk together about your views.

2 Monosyllables create a powerful dialogue (in pairs)

Short simple words can be charged with meaning and have great dramatic effect. Read lines 122–9 to each other, but accompany each monosyllabic word (a word with only one syllable) with a tap on the table or click of your fingers. How many words are not monosyllables? Work out a way of saying the lines so that they do not sound staccato (like the rat-a-tat-tat of a machine-gun). Try writing eight lines of dialogue in similar monosyllabic style.

3 'I am not what I am' – dramatic irony

In Shakespeare's time, line 126 would have been spoken by a boy playing a girl playing a boy. That fact made the words rich in dramatic irony (see p. 156). Today, Viola is played by a woman, but the line is still full of dramatic irony, because the audience knows what Olivia does not – the 'man' she is wooing is actually a woman.

---

hard construction harsh judgement
receiving perception
cypress thin linen
degree step
grise step
vulgar proof common experience

upbraids rebukes
westward ho! the cry of London boatmen offering to carry passengers from the City to Westminster (see p. 170)

Under your hard construction must I sit,   100
To force that on you in a shameful cunning
Which you knew none of yours. What might you think?
Have you not set mine honour at the stake,
And baited it with all th'unmuzzled thoughts
That tyrannous heart can think? To one of your receiving   105
Enough is shown; a cypress, not a bosom,
Hides my heart: so, let me hear you speak.

VIOLA I pity you.

OLIVIA   That's a degree to love.

VIOLA No, not a grise; for 'tis a vulgar proof
That very oft we pity enemies.   110

OLIVIA Why then, methinks 'tis time to smile again.
O world, how apt the poor are to be proud!
If one should be a prey, how much the better
To fall before the lion than the wolf!
(*Clock strikes*)
The clock upbraids me with the waste of time.   115
Be not afraid, good youth; I will not have you –
And yet when wit and youth is come to harvest,
Your wife is like to reap a proper man.
There lies your way, due west.

VIOLA   Then westward ho!
Grace and good disposition attend your ladyship!   120
You'll nothing, madam, to my lord by me?

OLIVIA Stay!
I prithee tell me what thou think'st of me.

VIOLA That you do think you are not what you are.

OLIVIA If I think so, I think the same of you.   125

VIOLA Then think you right: I am not what I am.

OLIVIA I would you were as I would have you be.

VIOLA Would it be better, madam, than I am?
I wish it might, for now I am your fool.

Olivia, admiring Viola's beauty and convinced that her own feelings are obvious, declares her love for Viola-Cesario. Viola swears that no woman has her heart except she herself.

Which line do you think is being spoken by Olivia (left)?

1 Should the rhymes be emphasised?

Lines 132–49 are rhyming couplets. Actors argue over whether they should emphasise the rhymes. To discover your views, take parts and speak the lines. First, emphasise the rhymes; in your second reading, don't. Which style do you feel actors should use on stage? It will help you to think of Olivia's lines 138–41 as 'Don't twist the fact that I'm wooing you to mean you shouldn't love me; but overcome that argument with this one ('reason thus with reason fetter'): loving is good, but receiving love is better.'

Love's night is noon love cannot be hidden, it will always shine out
maugre in spite of
extort extract
clause proposition

For that because
fetter chain up
deplore declare, complain about
abhors detests

OLIVIA [*Aside*] O what a deal of scorn looks beautiful   130
          In the contempt and anger of his lip!
          A murd'rous guilt shows not itself more soon,
          Than love that would seem hid. Love's night is noon.
          Cesario, by the roses of the spring,
          By maidhood, honour, truth, and everything,   135
          I love thee so that, maugre all thy pride,
          Nor wit nor reason can my passion hide.
          Do not extort thy reasons from this clause,
          For that I woo, thou therefore hast no cause;
          But rather reason thus with reason fetter: 140
          Love sought is good, but giv'n unsought is better.
VIOLA By innocence I swear, and by my youth,
          I have one heart, one bosom, and one truth,
          And that no woman has; nor never none
          Shall mistress be of it, save I alone.   145
          And so, adieu, good madam; never more
          Will I my master's tears to you deplore.
OLIVIA Yet come again: for thou perhaps mayst move
          That heart which now abhors to like his love.

                                                          Exeunt

Sir Andrew determines to leave because Olivia is paying more attention to Viola-Cesario. Fabian and Sir Toby persuade him to stay. He must challenge Viola-Cesario to a duel and so win Olivia's affection by his bravery.

What is Sir Andrew saying to Sir Toby at this moment?

1 Echoes of Elizabethan England

Shakespeare's audiences would have picked up references to recent events in the lines opposite (see also p. 170):

Lines 21–2 'hang like an icicle on a Dutchman's beard': Fabian compares Olivia's cold indifference and frosty disdain of Sir Andrew to a voyage to the Arctic made by a Dutchman, William Barents, in 1596–7.

Line 25 'Brownist': follower of an extreme puritan, Robert Brown.

venom fury
Marry by St Mary
great argument clear show
'Slight! by God's light
dormouse sleeping, timid
accosted greeted

fire-new from the mint like brand-new coins
balked let slip, neglected
double gilt twice goldplated
valour bravery
policy cunning, trickery
as lief as gladly

Act 3 Scene 2
A room in Olivia's house

Enter SIR TOBY, SIR ANDREW and FABIAN

SIR ANDREW No, faith, I'll not stay a jot longer!

SIR TOBY Thy reason, dear venom, give thy reason.

FABIAN You must needs yield your reason, Sir Andrew.

SIR ANDREW Marry, I saw your niece do more favours to the count's
servingman than ever she bestowed upon me. I saw't i'th'orchard.   5

SIR TOBY Did she see thee the while, old boy? Tell me that.

SIR ANDREW As plain as I see you now.

FABIAN This was a great argument of love in her toward you.

SIR ANDREW 'Slight! Will you make an ass o'me?

FABIAN I will prove it legitimate, sir, upon the oaths of judgement and   10
reason.

SIR TOBY And they have been grand-jurymen since before Noah was
a sailor.

FABIAN She did show favour to the youth in your sight only to
exasperate you, to awake your dormouse valour, to put fire in your   15
heart, and brimstone in your liver. You should then have accosted
her, and with some excellent jests, fire-new from the mint, you
should have banged the youth into dumbness. This was looked for
at your hand, and this was balked. The double gilt of this
opportunity you let time wash off, and you are now sailed into the   20
north of my lady's opinion, where you will hang like an icicle on
a Dutchman's beard unless you do redeem it by some laudable
attempt, either of valour or policy.

SIR ANDREW And't be any way, it must be with valour, for policy I
hate. I had as lief be a Brownist as a politician.   25

SIR TOBY Why then, build me thy fortunes upon the basis of valour.
Challenge me the count's youth to fight with him, hurt him in eleven
places – my niece shall take note of it – and assure thyself, there
is no love-broker in the world can more prevail in man's commen-
dation with woman than report of valour.   30

Sir Toby instructs Sir Andrew how to write the challenge in fierce, military language, but tells Fabian that Sir Andrew is a coward. Maria brings news that Malvolio has been transformed!

1 'Thou' and 'you' – showing relationships

To Elizabethans, words like 'thou', 'thy' and 'thee' were very significant. 'Thou' was used for a close friend, but was also used insultingly to someone you saw as an inferior (as Sir Toby advises in line 35). 'You' was a more formal way of speaking to someone. Check how Sir Toby and Fabian address Sir Andrew in this scene (as 'thou' or 'you'). How do you explain the difference?

2 Sir Toby: truth or trick? (in pairs)

Sir Toby is a mischief-maker. Although he pretends to be Sir Andrew's friend, he continually mocks and tricks him. But sometimes Sir Toby reveals his true thoughts (for instance, 'I have been dear to him' – I've spent his money). One person reads aloud everything Sir Toby says in this scene, a sentence at a time. Pause at the end of each sentence. The other person says either 'mischief' or 'truth' in each pause. Change roles and repeat.

3 More echoes of Shakespeare's England

- 'The bed of Ware' (line 37) was a huge bed that could sleep a dozen people. It is now in the Victoria and Albert Museum, London.
- 'the new map . . . Indies' (lines 62–3): a map of India and the Far East published in 1600. It had lines which radiated out from different points like wrinkles around the eyes.

Research one of these contemporary echoes or one of those on pages 80 or 170. Present your findings together with a comment on what you think such Elizabethan references add to the play.

---

curst fierce
invention imagination (or untruths)
goose-pen quill-pen (or cowardly)
cubiculo bedroom
dear manikin friendly puppet
wainropes wagon ropes
hale haul, drag

presage hint
spleen fit of laughter
gull dupe, tricked person
passages of grossness written
  nonsense
pedant schoolmaster

FABIAN There is no way but this, Sir Andrew.

SIR ANDREW Will either of you bear me a challenge to him?

SIR TOBY Go, write it in a martial hand, be curst and brief; it is no
matter how witty, so it be eloquent, and full of invention. Taunt
him with the licence of ink. If thou 'thou'st' him some thrice, it   35
shall not be amiss, and as many lies as will lie in thy sheet of paper,
although the sheet were big enough for the bed of Ware in England,
set 'em down. Go, about it! Let there be gall enough in thy ink;
though thou write with a goose-pen, no matter. About it!

SIR ANDREW Where shall I find you?   40

SIR TOBY We'll call thee at the cubiculo. Go!

Exit Sir Andrew

FABIAN This is a dear manikin to you, Sir Toby.

SIR TOBY I have been dear to him, lad, some two thousand strong, or
so.

FABIAN We shall have a rare letter from him, but you'll not deliver't?   45

SIR TOBY Never trust me then, and by all means stir on the youth to
an answer. I think oxen and wainropes cannot hale them together.
For Andrew, if he were opened and you find so much blood in his
liver as will clog the foot of a flea, I'll eat the rest of th'anatomy.

FABIAN And his opposite, the youth, bears in his visage no great presage 50
of cruelty.

Enter MARIA

SIR TOBY Look where the youngest wren of mine comes –

MARIA If you desire the spleen, and will laugh yourselves into stitches,
follow me. Yond gull Malvolio is turned heathen, a very renegado;
for there is no Christian that means to be saved by believing rightly   55
can ever believe such impossible passages of grossness. He's in
yellow stockings.

SIR TOBY And cross-gartered?

MARIA Most villainously. Like a pedant that keeps a school i'th'church.
I have dogged him like his murderer. He does obey every point of   60
the letter that I dropped to betray him. He does smile his face into
more lines than is in the new map with the augmentation of the
Indies; you have not seen such a thing as 'tis. I can hardly forbear
hurling things at him; I know my lady will strike him. If she do,
he'll smile and take't for a great favour.   65

SIR TOBY Come bring us, bring us where he is.

Exeunt

Antonio has followed Sebastian out of friendship and to protect him. Sebastian invites Antonio to join him in sightseeing. Antonio declines, fearing capture – he was once Orsino's enemy.

Sebastian (left) and Antonio. In Scene 3 Shakespeare shifts the audience's attention away from the love plot and the practical jokes being played on Malvolio and Sir Andrew. But these two characters will add yet more complications to the already tangled plots.

Choose a line from the script opposite which you think best fits this moment.

1 Advise the actors

Imagine the two actors ask your advice:

a 'When we look at lines 1–18, Antonio seems to care for Sebastian more than Sebastian cares for him. How should we play the lines?'

b 'Antonio is a wanted man in Illyria. How does he show by his manner that he's taking a considerable risk? How does Sebastian react to that manner?'

Write notes advising the actors on each point.

---

chide rebuke
jealousy fear
befall endanger
skilless in without knowledge
The rather the more speedily (the original meaning of 'rather')
shuffled off poorly rewarded

uncurrent worthless
relics famous buildings
the count his galleys Orsino's ships
tane captured (taken)
scarce be answered be difficult to avoid punishment

Act 3 Scene 3
A street

Enter SEBASTIAN and ANTONIO

SEBASTIAN I would not by my will have troubled you,
　　　　But since you make your pleasure of your pains,
　　　　I will no further chide you.
ANTONIO I could not stay behind you. My desire,
　　　　More sharp than filèd steel, did spur me forth;　　　　5
　　　　And not all love to see you (though so much
　　　　As might have drawn one to a longer voyage),
　　　　But jealousy what might befall your travel,
　　　　Being skilless in these parts which to a stranger,
　　　　Unguided, and unfriended, often prove　　　　10
　　　　Rough and unhospitable. My willing love,
　　　　The rather by these arguments of fear,
　　　　Set forth in your pursuit.
SEBASTIAN 　　　　　　　　My kind Antonio,
　　　　I can no other answer make but thanks,
　　　　And thanks, and ever thanks; and oft good turns　　　　15
　　　　Are shuffled off with such uncurrent pay;
　　　　But were my worth, as is my conscience, firm,
　　　　You should find better dealing. What's to do?
　　　　Shall we go see the relics of this town?
ANTONIO Tomorrow, sir; best first go see your lodging.　　　　20
SEBASTIAN I am not weary, and 'tis long to night.
　　　　I pray you, let us satisfy our eyes
　　　　With the memorials and the things of fame
　　　　That do renown this city.
ANTONIO 　　　　　　　　Would you'd pardon me.
　　　　I do not without danger walk these streets.　　　　25
　　　　Once in a sea-fight 'gainst the count his galleys
　　　　I did some service, of such note indeed
　　　　That were I tane here, it would scarce be answered.

Antonio is a wanted man in Illyria because he has not repaid what he captured in a sea-fight. He lends Sebastian money. The two men promise to meet later at the Elephant.

---

1 Antonio – a wanted man (in pairs)

Antonio is a wanted man in Illyria because of a sea-fight between the ships of his city and those of Duke Orsino. All his fellow citizens have made their peace by returning what they captured in the battle. Only Antonio has refused to settle. Choose one or more of the following:

a Design a 'wanted' poster of Antonio to be displayed on walls around Illyria.

b Write the Illyrian battle report of the sea-fight.

c Compile the official Illyrian document that records full details of Antonio's life.

d Take roles and speak the whole scene several times. Close the script and, in role, have a conversation trying to cover all they have said to each other. How much can you remember?

2 'The Elephant' – tell Shakespeare's story

The Elephant was an inn very close to the Globe Theatre. Shakespeare probably passed it every day on his way to the theatre. It has long since disappeared. The reference is not to the area of London now known as Elephant and Castle, because it was not called that in Shakespeare's time.

Was Shakespeare giving free publicity to the inn? Step into role as Shakespeare and write why you decided to use this name.

3 'I'll be your purse-bearer'

Watch out for the trouble that this loan of money (line 47) causes later in the play!

Belike perhaps	**beguile the time** pass the time
traffic's trade's	pleasantly
stood out did not pay	**Haply** maybe
lapsèd arrested	**toy** trifling object
It doth not fit me I'll be cautious	**store . . . markets** money is
bespeak our diet order our meal	insufficient for buying luxuries

SEBASTIAN Belike you slew great number of his people?
ANTONIO Th'offence is not of such a bloody nature,   30
       Albeit the quality of the time and quarrel
       Might well have given us bloody argument.
       It might have since been answered in repaying
       What we took from them, which for traffic's sake
       Most of our city did. Only myself stood out,   35
       For which if I be lapsèd in this place
       I shall pay dear.
SEBASTIAN   Do not then walk too open.
ANTONIO It doth not fit me. Hold, sir, here's my purse.
       In the south suburbs at the Elephant
       Is best to lodge; I will bespeak our diet,   40
       Whiles you beguile the time, and feed your knowledge
       With viewing of the town; there shall you have me.
SEBASTIAN Why I your purse?
ANTONIO Haply your eye shall light upon some toy
       You have desire to purchase; and your store,   45
       I think, is not for idle markets, sir.
SEBASTIAN I'll be your purse-bearer and leave you for
       An hour.
ANTONIO   To th'Elephant.
SEBASTIAN   I do remember.

Exeunt

Olivia is looking forward to Viola-Cesario's return, and thinking about how she will entertain 'him'. She sends for Malvolio, expecting him to be formal and sad. He appears – transformed and speaking very strangely!

1 Act it out! (in groups of six)

The first part of Scene 4 (lines 1–106) shows how the deluded Malvolio behaves towards Olivia, and what happens to him. It is one of the best-known and loved episodes in Shakespeare's plays. Malvolio's appearance in yellow stockings and cross-gartered is a great moment in every production. So the best thing to do is to act out the lines. Take parts as Olivia, Maria, Malvolio, the Servant, Sir Toby and Fabian and read lines 1–106 adding actions, gestures and expressions.

Remember, Malvolio is convinced that Olivia loves him. Olivia, knowing nothing of the forged letter, is astonished by his appearance and behaviour. The conspirators are beside themselves with glee, and are determined to add to the impression that Malvolio is mad. Get as much fun from the 'mis-takings' as you can!

2 She's talking about you!

Olivia makes a cynical remark about young people in line 3: 'For youth is bought more oft than begged or borrowed' (it's money that counts in winning young people's love). Do you share her view? Write your response to her remark, and say what it makes you think about her character – and her age.

3 'Please one, and please all'

Malvolio sings the opening lines of a popular Elizabethan song: 'The Crowe sits upon the Wall / Please one and please all'. Make up four lines to follow which express what's in Malvolio's mind at this moment.

---

bestow of him   give to him
possessed   mad, taken over by the
 devil
sonnet   song

black in my mind   melancholy
Roman hand   fashionable italic
 handwriting

Act 3 Scene 4
Olivia's garden

Enter OLIVIA followed by MARIA

OLIVIA [*Aside*] I have sent after him; he says he'll come –
How shall I feast him? What bestow of him?
For youth is bought more oft than begged or borrowed.
I speak too loud –
Where's Malvolio? He is sad and civil,   5
And suits well for a servant with my fortunes.
Where is Malvolio?

MARIA He's coming, madam, but in very strange manner. He is sure
possessed, madam.

OLIVIA Why, what's the matter? Does he rave?   10

MARIA No, madam, he does nothing but smile. Your ladyship were best
to have some guard about you, if he come, for sure the man is
tainted in's wits.

OLIVIA Go call him hither.

                                                              [*Exit Maria*]

                          I am as mad as he
If sad and merry madness equal be.   15

Enter [MARIA *with*] MALVOLIO

How now, Malvolio?

MALVOLIO Sweet lady, ho, ho!

OLIVIA Smil'st thou? I sent for thee upon a sad occasion.

MALVOLIO Sad, lady? I could be sad. This does make some obstruction
in the blood, this cross-gartering, but what of that? If it please the   20
eye of one, it is with me as the very true sonnet is: 'Please one,
and please all.'

OLIVIA Why, how dost thou, man? What is the matter with thee?

MALVOLIO Not black in my mind, though yellow in my legs. It did
come to his hands, and commands shall be executed. I think we   25
do know the sweet Roman hand.

Olivia is amazed by Malvolio's behaviour and appearance as he quotes the forged letter to her. She thinks he is mad, and gives orders for Sir Toby and others to look after him.

'Midsummer madness'. Malvolio shows off his yellow stockings.

1 Does she mean it?

What does the last sentence spoken by Olivia (lines 56–7) suggest to you about her true feelings for Malvolio?

To bed? Malvolio's surprised delight at what he thinks is Olivia's invitation should bring the house down!
daws jackdaws
restore cure

commended praised
thou art made you are blessed by fortune
could . . . entreat him back I had great difficulty keeping him out

OLIVIA Wilt thou go to bed, Malvolio?

MALVOLIO To bed? Ay, sweetheart, and I'll come to thee.

OLIVIA God comfort thee! Why dost thou smile so and kiss thy hand
    so oft?   30

MARIA How do you, Malvolio?

MALVOLIO At your request!
    Yes, nightingales answer daws!

MARIA Why appear you with this ridiculous boldness before my lady?

MALVOLIO 'Be not afraid of greatness': 'twas well writ.   35

OLIVIA What mean'st thou by that, Malvolio?

MALVOLIO 'Some are born great – '

OLIVIA Ha?

MALVOLIO 'Some achieve greatness – '

OLIVIA What say'st thou?   40

MALVOLIO 'And some have greatness thrust upon them.'

OLIVIA Heaven restore thee!

MALVOLIO 'Remember who commended thy yellow stockings – '

OLIVIA Thy yellow stockings?

MALVOLIO 'And wished to see thee cross-gartered.'   45

OLIVIA Cross-gartered?

MALVOLIO 'Go to, thou art made, if thou desir'st to be so – '

OLIVIA Am I made?

MALVOLIO 'If not, let me see thee a servant still.'

OLIVIA Why, this is very midsummer madness.   50

Enter SERVANT

SERVANT Madam, the young gentleman of the Count Orsino's is
    returned; I could hardly entreat him back. He attends your
    ladyship's pleasure.

OLIVIA I'll come to him.

                                                 [Exit Servant]

Good Maria, let this fellow be looked to. Where's my cousin Toby?   55
Let some of my people have a special care of him; I would not have
him miscarry for the half of my dowry.

                                 [Exeunt Olivia and Maria]

Malvolio convinces himself that what Olivia has just said means that she loves him. Following the letter's instructions, he is rude to Sir Toby, who accuses him of being possessed by devils.

1 Malvolio talks to himself (in small groups)

Malvolio's soliloquy (lines 58–73) works well as a 'conversation'. Sit in a circle. As Malvolio, each person takes a turn to read a sentence or phrase that reveals how pleased with himself Malvolio is. Add 'business' (gestures and action) to bring out his preening and vanity, and to increase the humour. Perhaps Malvolio hugs himself with joy, or takes out the letter and reads the extracts from it that he quotes.

2 Tormenting Malvolio (in groups of four)

In lines 74–106, Sir Toby, Fabian and Maria torment Malvolio with their mock concern. Take parts. The three conspirators stand around Malvolio. As each conspirator speaks, Malvolio turns away from them and replies contemptuously. Try other ways of heightening comic effect (e.g. Sir Toby could make signs to fend off the devil).

3 'Legion': the many devils who cause suffering

Sir Toby and Fabian are determined to treat Malvolio as if he is possessed by devils. 'Legion' (line 75) is mentioned in the Bible (St Mark's Gospel, chapter 5), where Jesus casts out a legion (a very great number) of devils from a madman. Some critics see the image as yet another way in which the play links suffering with love – Malvolio is accused of being mad because he believes that Olivia loves him. Which other characters in *Twelfth Night* suffer for love?

---

humble slough lowly appearance
tang talk pretentiously
singularity eccentricity
reverend carriage stately walk
limed caught (birds were trapped with lime)
Fellow companion (of Olivia)
degree rank (as a servant)

dram tiny weight
scruple even tinier weight (one third of a dram)
sanctity holiness
water urine
wise woman fortune teller (who claimed to be able to diagnose from urine samples)

MALVOLIO O ho, do you come near me now? No worse man than Sir
Toby to look to me! This concurs directly with the letter: she sends
him on purpose that I may appear stubborn to him; for she incites   60
me to that in the letter. 'Cast thy humble slough', says she; 'be
opposite with a kinsman, surly with servants, let thy tongue tang
with arguments of state, put thyself into the trick of singularity',
and consequently sets down the manner how: as a sad face, a
reverend carriage, a slow tongue, in the habit of some sir of note,   65
and so forth. I have limed her, but it is Jove's doing, and Jove make
me thankful! And when she went away now, 'Let this fellow be
looked to' – 'Fellow'! Not 'Malvolio', nor after my degree, but
'fellow'. Why, everything adheres together, that no dram of a
scruple, no scruple of a scruple, no obstacle, no incredulous or   70
unsafe circumstance – what can be said? Nothing that can be can
come between me and the full prospect of my hopes. Well, Jove,
not I, is the doer of this, and he is to be thanked!

Enter [SIR] TOBY, FABIAN, *and* MARIA

SIR TOBY Which way is he, in the name of sanctity? If all the devils
of hell be drawn in little, and Legion himself possessed him, yet   75
I'll speak to him.
FABIAN Here he is, here he is. How is't with you, sir?
SIR TOBY How is't with you, man?
MALVOLIO Go off, I discard you. Let me enjoy my private. Go off!
MARIA Lo, how hollow the fiend speaks within him! Did not I tell you?   80
Sir Toby, my lady prays you to have a care of him.
MALVOLIO Ah ha! Does she so?
SIR TOBY Go to, go to; peace, peace! We must deal gently with him.
Let me alone. How do you, Malvolio? How is't with you? What,
man, defy the devil! Consider, he's an enemy to mankind.   85
MALVOLIO Do you know what you say?
MARIA La you, and you speak ill of the devil, how he takes it at heart!
Pray God he be not bewitched!
FABIAN Carry his water to th'wise woman.
MARIA Marry, and it shall be done tomorrow morning if I live. My lady   90
would not lose him for more than I'll say.
MALVOLIO How now, mistress?
MARIA O Lord!

Sir Toby continues to pretend that Malvolio is mad. Malvolio refuses to be teased, and leaves. Sir Toby plans to tie him up and imprison him. Sir Andrew arrives with his letter of challenge to Viola-Cesario.

1 'Chuck', 'bawcock', 'biddy' = chicken!

Sir Toby treats Malvolio like a chicken, which has to be encouraged with 'pet' words, like 'bawcock' (fine bird), 'chuck' (chicken) and 'biddy' (chickabiddy). Invent stage business to accompany the lines. For example, does Sir Toby taunt Malvolio by clucking?

2 Identify Malvolio's feelings

Malvolio's language in lines 79–106 shows that he feels many different emotions as the others taunt him. Consider each of Malvolio's sentences in turn. For each, write down what Malvolio is feeling and thinking at that moment. Which sentence suggests that his religious feelings are greatly offended?

3 'If this were played upon a stage . . .' (in pairs)

In the theatre, Fabian's words (lines 108–9) should make the audience laugh. Talk together about what it is that makes the remark amusing. Then experiment with ways of speaking the lines to get the funniest effect. It helps if you consider how, and to whom Fabian says it: to the audience? to the others? to himself?

4 'In a dark room and bound' (in pairs)

Elizabethans believed that a mad person could be cured by tying them up and imprisoning them in a dark room. Sir Toby is keen to put this cruel 'cure' into practice with Malvolio. Talk together about what this suggests to you about Sir Toby's character, and how Maria and Fabian might react to the suggestion.

'tis not . . . Satan   dignified people shouldn't play children's games with the devil
foul collier   dirty digger
genius   soul, spirit
take air and taint   become known, and therefore spoiled

penance   confession
bar   court
More matter for a May morning!   More sport fit for a holiday!
keeps you from the blow of the law   saves you from prosecution

SIR TOBY Prithee, hold thy peace; this is not the way. Do you not see
    you move him? Let me alone with him.   95

FABIAN No way but gentleness; gently, gently: the fiend is rough, and
    will not be roughly used.

SIR TOBY Why, how now, my bawcock? How dost thou, chuck?

MALVOLIO Sir!

SIR TOBY Ay, biddy, come with me. What, man, 'tis not for gravity   100
    to play at cherry-pit with Satan. Hang him, foul collier!

MARIA Get him to say his prayers, good Sir Toby, get him to pray.

MALVOLIO My prayers, minx!

MARIA No, I warrant you, he will not hear of godliness.

MALVOLIO Go hang yourselves all! You are idle, shallow things; I am   105
    not of your element. You shall know more hereafter.   *Exit*

SIR TOBY Is't possible?

FABIAN If this were played upon a stage now, I could condemn it as
    an improbable fiction.

SIR TOBY His very genius hath taken the infection of the device, man.   110

MARIA Nay, pursue him now, lest the device take air and taint.

FABIAN Why, we shall make him mad indeed.

MARIA The house will be the quieter.

SIR TOBY Come, we'll have him in a dark room and bound. My niece
    is already in the belief that he's mad. We may carry it thus for our   115
    pleasure, and his penance, till our very pastime, tired out of breath,
    prompt us to have mercy on him; at which time we will bring the
    device to the bar and crown thee for a finder of madmen. But see,
    but see!

Enter SIR ANDREW

FABIAN More matter for a May morning!   120

SIR ANDREW Here's the challenge; read it. I warrant there's vinegar
    and pepper in't.

FABIAN Is't so saucy?

SIR ANDREW Ay, is't. I warrant him; do but read.

SIR TOBY Give me. [*Reads*] 'Youth, whatsoever thou art, thou art but   125
    a scurvy fellow.'

FABIAN Good, and valiant.

SIR TOBY [*Reads*] 'Wonder not, nor admire not in thy mind, why I do
    call thee so, for I will show thee no reason for't.'

FABIAN A good note! That keeps you from the blow of the law.   130

Sir Toby reads Sir Andrew's contorted letter and orders him to challenge Viola-Cesario forcefully in the orchard. Sir Andrew leaves, and Sir Toby reveals he plans to trick both duellists into mutual fright.

---

1 Write Sir Andrew's challenge

The first audience for *Twelfth Night* probably included many law students (see p. 174). They would relish Sir Andrew's attempts to ensure that his letter doesn't land him in court ('keep o'th'windy side of the law'). Write out Sir Andrew's challenge to Viola-Cesario. Try to make the handwriting reveal Sir Andrew's true feelings. As a knight, Sir Andrew might also sketch his coat of arms for added effect.

2 'Thou', 'thee' and 'thy'

Earlier, Sir Toby urged Sir Andrew to use 'thou' when writing to Viola-Cesario (Act 3 Scene 2, lines 35–6). Read the letter aloud emphasising every 'thou', 'thy' and 'thee'. Turn back to page 82 to remind yourself of the Elizabethan custom about the use of 'thou'.

3 'Like cockatrices' (in pairs)

Cockatrices were mythical serpents, supposed to be able to kill with a look (line 163). Show your partner how to kill like a cockatrice.

4 Sir Toby relishes another trick (in pairs)

Sir Toby is up to no good yet again. He wants to further humiliate his friend, Sir Andrew. He plans to trick both Sir Andrew and Viola-Cesario into believing that the other is a superb swordsman, so that they will be terrified of each other. Take turns to speak Sir Toby's plot in lines 154–63. Put as much malicious glee into your voices as possible.

---

o'th'windy side of the law safe from prosecution
commerce conversation, business
bumbaily bailiff (who approached from behind)
approbation credit

of good capacity and breeding intelligent and noble
clodpole blockhead
set upon attribute to, give
presently immediately
horrid threatening

SIR TOBY [*Reads*] 'Thou com'st to the Lady Olivia, and in my sight she uses thee kindly. But thou liest in thy throat. That is not the matter I challenge thee for.'

FABIAN Very brief, and to exceeding good sense [*Aside*] – less.

SIR TOBY [*Reads*] 'I will waylay thee going home, where if it be thy   135
chance to kill me –'

FABIAN Good.

SIR TOBY [*Reads*] 'Thou kill'st me like a rogue and a villain.'

FABIAN Still you keep o'th'windy side of the law. Good.

SIR TOBY [*Reads*] 'Fare thee well, and God have mercy upon one of   140
our souls! He may have mercy upon mine, but my hope is better,
and so look to thyself. Thy friend, as thou usest him, and thy sworn
enemy,

Andrew Aguecheek.'

If this letter move him not, his legs cannot. I'll give't him.   145

MARIA You may have very fit occasion for't; he is now in some
commerce with my lady and will by and by depart.

SIR TOBY Go, Sir Andrew, scout me for him at the corner of the orchard
like a bumbaily. So soon as ever thou seest him, draw, and as thou
draw'st, swear horrible; for it comes to pass oft that a terrible oath,   150
with a swaggering accent sharply twanged off, gives manhood more
approbation than ever proof itself would have earned him. Away!

SIR ANDREW Nay, let me alone for swearing.   *Exit*

SIR TOBY Now will not I deliver his letter; for the behaviour of the
young gentleman gives him out to be of good capacity and breeding;   155
his employment between his lord and my niece confirms no less.
Therefore this letter, being so excellently ignorant, will breed no
terror in the youth; he will find it comes from a clodpole. But, sir,
I will deliver his challenge by word of mouth, set upon Aguecheek
a notable report of valour, and drive the gentleman (as I know his   160
youth will aptly receive it) into a most hideous opinion of his rage,
skill, fury, and impetuosity. This will so fright them both that they
will kill one another by the look, like cockatrices.

FABIAN Here he comes with your niece; give them way till he take leave
and presently after him.   165

Enter OLIVIA *and* VIOLA

SIR TOBY I will meditate the while upon some horrid message for a
challenge.

[*Exeunt Sir Toby, Fabian, and Maria*]

Olivia reveals her passionate love to Viola-Cesario, and gives 'him' a jewel. Viola-Cesario tells her to love Orsino instead. Sir Toby tells Viola-Cesario to draw 'his' sword and face Sir Andrew's rage and supreme swordsmanship.

1 A brief 'love' episode (in pairs)

The brief episode in which Olivia and Viola talk together is a reminder of the absurdity of Olivia's love. It is also a kind of 'dramatic bridge' to continue the comic plot, ensuring that Viola will be drawn into Sir Toby's malicious scheme. Take parts, speak lines 168–84, and then work on the following activities:

a At the opening of the scene, Olivia was impatiently awaiting the arrival of Viola-Cesario. Now she enters with 'I have said too much unto a heart of stone' (line 168), and says that she has spoken without caution ('unchary') of her love for 'him'. Improvise the offstage conversation in which Olivia again reveals her love, but Viola-Cesario rejects it.

b Just what kind of 'jewel' does Olivia give? The clue is in line 175.

c Talk together about whether Shakespeare might have first written 'fiend' instead of 'friend' in line 184. Which word do you prefer – and why?

d Decide on a dramatically effective way for Olivia to leave.

2 The comic plot develops! (in pairs)

The next episode in Scene 4 presents the comic preparations for the 'duel' between Viola and Sir Andrew (lines 185–263). First, Sir Toby paints a picture of a furious and formidable Sir Andrew (lines 185–219). Viola is puzzled and probably frightened.

Take parts and read the lines. Change roles and read through again with Viola trying to get away from Sir Toby while he constantly pursues her, emphasising all the violent words.

With the same 'haviour . . . griefs Orsino suffers in similar manner
acquit release
betake thee to't prepare it
Dismount thy tuck unsheath your rapier
yare quick
opposite opponent, enemy

dubbed with unhatched rapier made a knight with an unused (unhacked) sword
carpet consideration non-military service
sepulchre burial
Hob nob have or have not (kill or be killed)

OLIVIA I have said too much unto a heart of stone,
      And laid mine honour too unchary on't;
      There's something in me that reproves my fault,   170
      But such a headstrong potent fault it is,
      That it but mocks reproof.
VIOLA With the same 'haviour that your passion bears
      Goes on my master's griefs.
OLIVIA Here, wear this jewel for me; 'tis my picture.   175
      Refuse it not; it hath no tongue to vex you.
      And, I beseech you, come again tomorrow.
      What shall you ask of me that I'll deny,
      That honour, saved, may upon asking give?
VIOLA Nothing but this – your true love for my master.   180
OLIVIA How with mine honour may I give him that
      Which I have given to you?
VIOLA   I will acquit you.
OLIVIA Well, come again tomorrow. Fare thee well.
      A friend like thee might bear my soul to hell.   *[Exit]*

Enter SIR TOBY *and* FABIAN

SIR TOBY Gentleman, God save thee.   185
VIOLA And you, sir.
SIR TOBY That defence thou hast, betake thee to't. Of what nature the
    wrongs are thou hast done him, I know not; but thy intercepter, full
    of despite, bloody as the hunter, attends thee at the orchard-end.
    Dismount thy tuck, be yare in thy preparation, for thy assailant is   190
    quick, skilful, and deadly.
VIOLA You mistake, sir. I am sure no man hath any quarrel to me. My
    remembrance is very free and clear from any image of offence done
    to any man.
SIR TOBY You'll find it otherwise, I assure you. Therefore, if you hold   195
    your life at any price, betake you to your guard; for your opposite
    hath in him what youth, strength, skill, and wrath can furnish man
    withal.
VIOLA I pray you, sir, what is he?
SIR TOBY He is knight, dubbed with unhatched rapier, and on carpet   200
    consideration, but he is a devil in private brawl. Souls and bodies
    hath he divorced three, and his incensement at this moment is so
    implacable that satisfaction can be none but by pangs of death and
    sepulchre. Hob nob is his word: give't or take't.

Viola tries to avoid the duel, but Sir Toby, then Fabian, prevent her and tell of Sir Andrew's anger and bravery. Sir Toby then similarly frightens Sir Andrew with report of Viola's sword-fencing skill.

---

1 Sir Andrew: how he's described – and what he is!

Collect all the words in lines 185–231 which describe Sir Andrew. Copy out and complete the diagram below, putting his name in the centre of a large piece of paper and writing the words from the script around it.

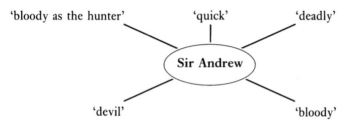

Under each description write other words which you think describe him more accurately. You can use words and phrases from other parts of the play if you wish.

2 'He has been fencer to the sophy'

In 1600, Sir Anthony Sherley published an account of his adventures whilst serving as ambassador to the shah of Persia ('the sophy'). Elizabethans were fascinated by the story. Shakespeare probably put in this reference to amuse the audience. Sir Anthony's brother, Robert, was still serving in the shah's army when the play was written.

Write a sentence describing the image that comes into Sir Andrew's mind when he hears the expression 'fencer to the sophy'.

---

conduct safety
quirk peculiarity, type
competent sufficient, real
meddle get involved
iron sword
mortal arbitrement fight to the death

read him by his form judge by his appearance
mettle bravery
firago virago (female warrior)
mortal motion fatal thrust
Pox on't curse it

VIOLA I will return again into the house and desire some conduct of   205
the lady. I am no fighter. I have heard of some kind of men that
put quarrels purposely on others to taste their valour; belike this
is a man of that quirk.

SIR TOBY Sir, no. His indignation derives itself out of a very competent
injury; therefore get you on and give him his desire. Back you shall   210
not to the house, unless you undertake that with me which with
as much safety you might answer him; therefore on, or strip your
sword stark naked; for meddle you must, that's certain, or forswear
to wear iron about you.

VIOLA This is as uncivil as strange. I beseech you, do me this courteous   215
office as to know of the knight what my offence to him is. It is
something of my negligence, nothing of my purpose.

SIR TOBY I will do so. Signior Fabian, stay you by this gentleman till
my return.   *Exit [Sir] Toby*

VIOLA Pray you, sir, do you know of this matter?   220

FABIAN I know the knight is incensed against you, even to a mortal
arbitrement, but nothing of the circumstance more.

VIOLA I beseech you, what manner of man is he?

FABIAN Nothing of that wonderful promise, to read him by his form,
as you are like to find him in the proof of his valour. He is indeed,   225
sir, the most skilful, bloody, and fatal opposite that you could
possibly have found in any part of Illyria. Will you walk towards
him? I will make your peace with him if I can.

VIOLA I shall be much bound to you for't. I am one that had rather
go with sir priest than sir knight. I care not who knows so much   230
of my mettle.

Exeunt

Enter [SIR] TOBY *and* [SIR] ANDREW

SIR TOBY Why, man, he's a very devil. I have not seen such a firago.
I had a pass with him, rapier, scabbard, and all, and he gives me
the stuck-in with such a mortal motion that it is inevitable; and on
the answer, he pays you as surely as your feet hits the ground they   235
step on. They say he has been fencer to the sophy.

SIR ANDREW Pox on't. I'll not meddle with him.

SIR TOBY Ay, but he will not now be pacified. Fabian can scarce hold
him yonder.

Andrew promises to give Sir Toby his horse if he can persuade Viola-Cesario to call off the duel. Viola is equally terrified. Sir Toby forces them to draw swords, but Antonio enters and intervenes on Viola's behalf.

1 Stage the duel – bring out the humour (in small groups)

Lines 220–63 make wonderfully funny theatre. Both Viola and Sir Andrew are terrified of each other. Fabian and Sir Toby do all they can to heighten the fear. Sometimes the mock fight lasts for several minutes as the petrified opponents, spurred on by Sir Toby and Fabian, ludicrously fence with each other. In some productions, they cover their eyes and jump back fearfully at any touch of swords. Viola speaks an Aside (lines 255–6) which, with its irony and sexual humour (see below), usually causes great audience amusement.

Take parts (have a director if you wish) and work out how to stage the lines for maximum comic effect. Safety warning: don't use real swords or sharp objects!

---

motion offer
perdition of souls loss of life
Marry by St Mary
conceited full of imagined fear
supportance of his vow obedience to
  the rules of duelling

little thing / lack of a man (a penis)
duello rules of duelling
undertaker someone who meddles in
  another's affairs

SIR ANDREW Plague on't, and I thought he had been valiant, and so 240
cunning in fence, I'd have seen him damned ere I'd have challenged
him. Let him let the matter slip, and I'll give him my horse, Grey
Capilet.

SIR TOBY I'll make the motion. Stand here, make a good show on't.
This shall end without the perdition of souls. [*Aside*] Marry, I'll 245
ride your horse as well as I ride you.

Enter FABIAN *and* VIOLA

[*To Fabian*] I have his horse to take up the quarrel. I have
persuaded him the youth's a devil.

FABIAN He is as horribly conceited of him and pants and looks pale,
as if a bear were at his heels. 250

SIR TOBY [*To Viola*] There's no remedy, sir. He will fight with you
for's oath sake. Marry, he hath better bethought him of his quarrel,
and he finds that now scarce to be worth talking of. Therefore, draw
for the supportance of his vow. He protests he will not hurt you.

VIOLA [*Aside*] Pray God defend me! A little thing would make me tell 255
them how much I lack of a man.

FABIAN Give ground if you see him furious.

SIR TOBY Come, Sir Andrew, there's no remedy: the gentleman will
for his honour's sake have one bout with you; he cannot by the
duello avoid it, but he has promised me, as he is a gentleman and 260
a soldier, he will not hurt you. Come on, to't.

SIR ANDREW Pray God he keep his oath!

VIOLA I do assure you, 'tis against my will.
[*They draw*]

Enter ANTONIO

ANTONIO [*Drawing*] Put up your sword! If this young gentleman
Have done offence, I take the fault on me; 265
If you offend him, I for him defy you.

SIR TOBY You, sir? Why, what are you?

ANTONIO One, sir, that for his love dares yet do more
Than you have heard him brag to you he will.

SIR TOBY Nay, if you be an undertaker, I am for you. [*Draws*] 270

Enter OFFICERS

FABIAN O good Sir Toby, hold! Here comes the officers.

Viola-Cesario and Sir Andrew make peace. The officers arrest Antonio. He asks Viola-Cesario for his money, mistaking 'him' for Sebastian. Puzzled, she offers him half her own small amount of money. He expresses disappointment at her apparent ingratitude.

---

1 'You stand amazed'

Shakespeare often builds stage directions into characters' language. It's no wonder that Viola is bewildered. First she finds herself forced into a duel for no reason she can discover. Then Sir Andrew says something very odd to her, promising her a horse (lines 274–5) she knows nothing about. Now her rescuer, a man she has never seen before, is arrested and asks her to return his money!

Work through lines 274–90 (in which Viola does not speak). Write suggestions as to how Viola could react to each line or phrase.

2 Betrayed by a friend (in pairs)

Antonio mistakes Viola–Cesario for Sebastian. Antonio's incredulity at his friend's apparent ingratitude is yet another 'episode' in Scene 4 which lends itself to acting out. Take parts as Viola and Antonio and speak lines 282–323 (leave out the Officers' lines). Try to express Antonio's disappointment and increasing anger, and Viola's bewilderment.

3 'I hate ingratitude' (in small groups)

Shakespeare seems to have hated ingratitude (not being grateful for kindnesses done for you). He refers to it very critically in several plays (*Coriolanus*, *King Lear*, *Troilus and Cressida*). Now Antonio accuses Viola of ingratitude. Do you share Viola's judgement (lines 305–8) that ingratitude is more hateful than any other vice? Begin by talking together about the other three vices she mentions.

---

anon immediately		**coffer** purse	
reins well handles well		**deserts** claims for past kindnesses	
office duty		**unsound** mean-spirited	
suit order		**upbraid** rebuke	
favour features, appearance		**vainness** boasting	
my present my money			

SIR TOBY [*To Antonio*] I'll be with you anon.

VIOLA [*To Sir Andrew*] Pray, sir, put your sword up, if you please.

SIR ANDREW Marry, will I, sir; and for that I promised you, I'll be
    as good as my word. He will bear you easily and reins well. 275

1 OFFICER This is the man; do thy office.

2 OFFICER Antonio, I arrest thee at the suit
    Of Count Orsino.

ANTONIO   You do mistake me, sir.

1 OFFICER No, sir, no jot. I know your favour well,
    Though now you have no sea-cap on your head. 280
    Take him away; he knows I know him well.

ANTONIO I must obey. [*To Viola*] This comes with seeking you.
    But there's no remedy; I shall answer it.
    What will you do, now my necessity
    Makes me to ask you for my purse? It grieves me 285
    Much more for what I cannot do for you
    Than what befalls myself. You stand amazed,
    But be of comfort.

2 OFFICER Come, sir, away.

ANTONIO I must entreat of you some of that money. 290

VIOLA What money, sir?
    For the fair kindness you have showed me here,
    And part being prompted by your present trouble,
    Out of my lean and low ability
    I'll lend you something. My having is not much; 295
    I'll make division of my present with you.
    Hold, there's half my coffer.

ANTONIO Will you deny me now?
    Is't possible that my deserts to you
    Can lack persuasion? Do not tempt my misery, 300
    Lest that it make me so unsound a man
    As to upbraid you with those kindnesses
    That I have done for you.

VIOLA   I know of none,
    Nor know I you by voice or any feature.
    I hate ingratitude more in a man 305
    Than lying, vainness, babbling drunkenness,
    Or any taint of vice whose strong corruption
    Inhabits our frail blood.

Antonio reflects that good looks can hide a bad character. He is led away to prison. Viola hopes that Antonio's mistake means that her brother is still alive. Sir Andrew vows to beat Viola. Sir Toby is unimpressed.

1 Putting Sebastian on a pedestal (in small groups)

Antonio has clearly put Sebastian on a pedestal, worshipping him like a god ('sanctity', 'image', 'venerable', 'devotion', 'idol', 'god'). Talk together about how Antonio's 'religious' language adds to your impression of his friendship with Sebastian.

2 Appearance versus reality: 'beauteous-evil' (in small groups)

Antonio's four lines (318–21) are yet another example of the play's theme of appearance versus reality. Antonio reflects that only an unkind nature can be called 'deformed'. Wickedness can hide behind good looks ('beauteous-evil').

• Turn back to Act 1 Scene 2, lines 48–51. You will find that Viola says something very similar.
• Do you agree with Antonio? Talk together about whether it is possible to judge what someone is really like from their outward appearance.

3 Rhyming couplets = 'sage saws'?

Sir Toby mocks rhyming couplets which express generalisations ('sage saws', lines 328–9). His sarcastic remark is probably prompted by his overhearing some or all of Antonio's and Viola's speeches. Identify the seven rhyming couplets in the script opposite.

4 Write the official report (in pairs)

Give the Officers a voice. Write their report on all they saw and heard in lines 271–323.

Relieved saved
sanctity holiness, sacredness
venerable worth deserving (of) devotion
trunks bodies
o'er-flourished overdressed
tane mistaken

sage saws wise sayings
Yet living in my glass is the mirror image of me
favour appearance, feature
Still always
paltry contemptible, mean
'Slid by God's eyelid

ANTONIO   O heavens themselves!

2 OFFICER Come, sir, I pray you go.

ANTONIO Let me speak a little. This youth that you see here,   310
          I snatched one-half out of the jaws of death,
          Relieved him with such sanctity of love;
          And to his image, which methought did promise
          Most venerable worth, did I devotion.

1 OFFICER What's that to us? The time goes by. Away!   315

ANTONIO But O how vile an idol proves this god!
          Thou hast, Sebastian, done good feature shame.
          In nature there's no blemish but the mind:
          None can be called deformed but the unkind.
          Virtue is beauty, but the beauteous-evil   320
          Are empty trunks, o'er-flourished by the devil.

1 OFFICER The man grows mad. Away with him! Come, come, sir.

ANTONIO Lead me on.

                                        Exit [*with Officers*]

VIOLA Methinks his words do from such passion fly
          That he believes himself; so do not I.   325
          Prove true, imagination, O prove true,
          That I, dear brother, be now tane for you!

SIR TOBY Come hither, knight, come hither, Fabian. We'll whisper o'er
          a couplet or two of most sage saws.

VIOLA He named Sebastian. I my brother know   330
          Yet living in my glass; even such and so
          In favour was my brother, and he went
          Still in this fashion, colour, ornament,
          For him I imitate. O if it prove,
          Tempests are kind, and salt waves fresh in love.   [*Exit*]   335

SIR TOBY A very dishonest paltry boy, and more a coward than a hare;
          his dishonesty appears in leaving his friend here in necessity, and
          denying him; and for his cowardship, ask Fabian.

FABIAN A coward, a most devout coward, religious in it.

SIR ANDREW 'Slid, I'll after him again and beat him.   340

SIR TOBY Do, cuff him soundly, but never draw thy sword.

SIR ANDREW And I do not –   [*Exit*]

FABIAN Come, let's see the event.

SIR TOBY I dare lay any money, 'twill be nothing yet.

                                        Exeunt

Looking back at Act 3
Activities for groups or individuals

---

1 Appearance versus reality

The theme of appearance versus reality is very obvious throughout Act 3. Nearly every character is deceived by outward appearance. Make a list of the characters who appear in the act. Alongside each name write who or what they have mistaken. You will find that Sir Andrew mistakes just about everyone!

2 Can you hide your feelings?

Olivia is convinced that love, like guilt, shows itself clearly in a person's face and behaviour. In Scene 1, line 133 she says, 'Love's night is noon' (love cannot be hidden).

Do you agree? Will love always show itself clearly? Using examples from your own experience, talk together about whether you think your deepest feelings can remain private to you and hidden from others.

3 Compile a tourist guide to Illyria

In Scene 3, line 19 Sebastian sounds like a tourist: 'Shall we go see the relics of this town?' Imagine that Illyria possesses a tourist office. What would its official guide say about the historic monuments of the town? Design a publicity pamphlet for Illyria. Remember that in line 11 of Scene 3, Antonio says that Illyria can be a 'Rough and unhospitable' place. So there are things the tourist office would want to hide, or to describe euphemistically (describing harsh or unpleasant things in mild or vague terms). Pages 168–70 may help you.

4 Should she speak to the audience?

Viola, as Cesario, speaks many lines which are full of dramatic irony. The audience knows she is a woman, but everyone on stage thinks she is a man. Talk together about whether or not Viola should acknowledge the audience in any way when she speaks such lines. For example, in Scene 4, lines 255–6 she says, 'A little thing would make me tell them how much I lack of a man.' The lines usually raise a laugh, but do you think she should say them directly to the audience? Would it be out of character?

Opponents in love The duel brings together two lovers. Sir Andrew wants to woo Olivia, and thinks that Viola-Cesario is wooing her too. He does not suspect that Viola-Cesario is a woman who loves Orsino. Make two lists. The first identifies what Sir Andrew has in common with Viola, and the second list sets out their differences.

Feste has mistaken Sebastian for Viola. Sebastian tries to get rid of him with money and a threat. Sir Andrew makes the same mistake, strikes Sebastian – and is hit in return!

---

1 Mistaken identity: 'Nothing that is so is so' (in small groups)

Scene 1 opens with yet another example of mistaken identity: Feste thinks Sebastian is Viola-Cesario. Feste's words could be the motto of the play. They express the theme of appearance versus reality: appearances are deceptive. As the scene develops, Sir Andrew, Sir Toby and Olivia will also mistake Sebastian for Viola-Cesario. For their mistakes:

- Feste receives money and the threat of a beating
- Sir Andrew gets a beating
- Sir Toby almost fights a duel
- Olivia seems about to get the man of her dreams.

a Take parts as Feste, Sebastian, Sir Andrew, Sir Toby and Olivia and read the whole scene. As you speak lines 1–20, try to bring out Sebastian's increasing irritation, and Feste's conviction that he is speaking to Cesario.

b Work out how Sir Toby and Sir Andrew enter (Fabian does not speak in the scene), and how Sebastian responds to being hit. Remember – safety first! No one must actually be struck. Actors use techniques (like clapping their hands as their opponent pretends to strike) to persuade the audience that an actual blow is struck.

2 'Foolish Greek' = don't speak double-Dutch

In Shakespeare's day, 'Greek' (line 15) was used to describe unintelligible language. Even today, people say 'It's all Greek to me' when they hear something they don't understand. A similar expression is 'double-Dutch'. You can find the origin of the expression 'It's all Greek to me' in Shakespeare's *Julius Caesar*, Act 1 Scene 2, line 273.

---

vent thy folly get rid of your foolishness
lubber awkward fool
cockney spoilt child, affected speaker
ungird thy strangeness stop pretending you don't know me

By my troth truly
open hand ready to give money (or to strike)
after fourteen years' purchase for a great deal of money (in Elizabethan England the price of land was equal to twelve years' rent)

Act 4 Scene 1
The street outside Olivia's house

Enter SEBASTIAN and FESTE

FESTE Will you make me believe that I am not sent for you?

SEBASTIAN Go to, go to, thou art a foolish fellow.
Let me be clear of thee.

FESTE Well held out, i'faith! No, I do not know you, nor I am not sent
to you by my lady to bid you come speak with her; nor your name   5
is not Master Cesario; nor this is not my nose neither. Nothing that
is so is so.

SEBASTIAN I prithee, vent thy folly somewhere else.
Thou know'st not me.

FESTE Vent my folly! He has heard that word of some great man and   10
now applies it to a fool. Vent my folly! I am afraid this great lubber
the world will prove a cockney. I prithee now, ungird thy
strangeness and tell me what I shall vent to my lady. Shall I vent
to her that thou art coming?

SEBASTIAN I prithee, foolish Greek, depart from me.   15
There's money for thee. If you tarry longer,
I shall give worse payment.

FESTE By my troth, thou hast an open hand. These wise men that give
fools money get themselves a good report – after fourteen years'
purchase.   20

Enter [SIR] ANDREW, [SIR] TOBY, *and* FABIAN

SIR ANDREW Now, sir, have I met you again? There's for you!
[*Strikes Sebastian*]

SEBASTIAN Why, there's for thee, and there, and there!
[*Beats Sir Andrew*]
Are all the people mad?

SIR TOBY Hold, sir, or I'll throw your dagger o'er the house.

Sir Toby challenges Sebastian to a fight, but Olivia intervenes and orders Sir Toby and his friends to leave. She invites Sebastian to go with her. He willingly agrees, wondering if it is all a dream.

1 Sebastian's point of view

Consider the scene from Sebastian's point of view. First, he meets a fool who calls him 'Cesario' and talks incomprehensibly about an invitation from a lady. Then he is assaulted by one man and threatened by another. Finally, a beautiful woman invites him lovingly into her house. No wonder he thinks he's either mad or dreaming – and wants to continue dreaming! ('Let fancy still . . . in Lethe steep' means 'Let love always plunge my reason in the river of forgetfulness'.)

a Write Sebastian's diary describing the events of the scene.

b Draw a graph, diagram or flow chart, plotting the events of the scene and the changes of Sebastian's mood.

2 Typical language

Write the name of each character who speaks in Scene 1. Alongside each name write one sentence, line or phrase they speak which you think expresses their personality. Which character's language did you find easiest to choose? And which was hardest? Suggest why.

3 Make a grand entrance! (in pairs)

Olivia's lines 38–44 give every actor a tremendous opportunity to play the grand lady. Some productions give her a stately entrance, but in the 2002 production at the Globe Theatre (see pp. 176–7), she charged on carrying an enormous spear! Experiment with saying the lines to each other in the most powerful way you can. Add appropriate gestures. Remember, at this moment Olivia must totally command the stage.

---

action of battery summons for assault
put up your iron draw your sword
well fleshed experienced in bloodshed
malapert saucy
sway rule

uncivil and unjust extent boisterous and lawless assault
botched up clumsily carried out
Beshrew curse
He started . . . in thee he made my heart leap with fear
relish meaning

FESTE This will I tell my lady straight; I would not be in some of your   25
    coats for twopence.   [*Exit*]
SIR TOBY Come on, sir, hold!
SIR ANDREW Nay, let him alone. I'll go another way to work with him;
    I'll have an action of battery against him, if there be any law in
    Illyria. Though I struck him first, yet it's no matter for that.   30
SEBASTIAN Let go thy hand!
SIR TOBY Come, sir, I will not let you go. Come, my young soldier,
    put up your iron. You are well fleshed. Come on!
SEBASTIAN I will be free from thee. [*Draws his sword*] What wouldst
    thou now?
    If thou dar'st tempt me further, draw thy sword.   35
SIR TOBY What, what! Nay, then, I must have an ounce or two of this
    malapert blood from you. [*Draws*]

                Enter OLIVIA

OLIVIA Hold, Toby! On thy life I charge thee hold!
SIR TOBY Madam –
OLIVIA Will it be ever thus? Ungracious wretch,   40
    Fit for the mountains and the barbarous caves,
    Where manners ne'er were preached! Out of my sight!
    Be not offended, dear Cesario.
    Rudesby, be gone!
                [*Exeunt Sir Toby, Sir Andrew, and Fabian*]
    I prithee, gentle friend,
    Let thy fair wisdom, not thy passion, sway   45
    In this uncivil and unjust extent
    Against thy peace. Go with me to my house
    And hear thou there how many fruitless pranks
    This ruffian hath botched up, that thou thereby
    Mayst smile at this. Thou shalt not choose but go.   50
    Do not deny. Beshrew his soul for me,
    He started one poor heart of mine, in thee.
SEBASTIAN What relish is in this? How runs the stream?
    Or I am mad, or else this is a dream.
    Let fancy still my sense in Lethe steep;   55
    If it be thus to dream, still let me sleep!
OLIVIA Nay, come, I prithee; would thou'dst be ruled by me!
SEBASTIAN Madam, I will.
OLIVIA   O say so, and so be!
                                            Exeunt

Maria encourages Feste to disguise himself as Sir Topas, the curate. He jokes with Sir Toby, and then begins to torment the imprisoned Malvolio, treating Malvolio as if he were mad.

1 How to show Malvolio 'in a dark room'?

Scene 2 stages further humiliation of Malvolio. All kinds of sets have been used to show his imprisonment. He has been chained like a bear to a stake, and caged like a lion. In one production, only his hands were seen through a grill (also see pictures on pp. xi (bottom), 118 and 178).

Design a set that includes a 'dark room' as Malvolio's prison. Ensure the audience can understand what's going on.

2 Making nonsense seem impressive (in pairs)

In Elizabethan times, priests like Sir Topas were regarded as great scholars. But they also became the subject of many jokes. Feste parodies the academic style of churchmen, using pretentious language and mock logic. He invents fictitious experts ('the old hermit of Prague') and imitates philosophical talk ('That that is, is'). In the previous scene, Feste said 'Nothing that is so is so'. So now he says just the opposite! It's all part of the topsy-turvy world of Illyria, where appearances are deceptive and all things are possible – or impossible!

a Take turns to speak lines 11–14 as if you were an old, learned professor, talking of very important truths.

b Invent another short speech for Feste in the same style of high-sounding nonsense as in lines 11–14.

Shakespeare may also be making fun of the Church here, just as he does in lines 4–9: 'dissembled' (deceived), 'tall' (able to see over the pulpit), 'great scholar' (which he makes equal to 'good housekeeper').

---

dissemble disguise, conceal my true identity
function role as priest
competitors conspirators
Bonos dies good day (bad Latin)

King Gorboduc legendary king of Britain
hyperbolical fantastical (exaggerated)
vexest thou you torment
use greet

Act 4 Scene 2
A room in Olivia's house

Enter MARIA *and* FESTE

MARIA Nay, I prithee put on this gown and this beard; make him
believe thou art Sir Topas the curate. Do it quickly. I'll call Sir
Toby the whilst. *[Exit]*

FESTE Well, I'll put it on, and I will dissemble myself in't, and I would
I were the first that ever dissembled in such a gown. I am not tall   5
enough to become the function well, nor lean enough to be thought
a good student; but to be said an honest man and a good
housekeeper goes as fairly as to say a careful man and a great
scholar. The competitors enter.

Enter [SIR] TOBY [*and* MARIA]

SIR TOBY Jove bless thee, Master Parson.   10

FESTE *Bonos dies*, Sir Toby. For as the old hermit of Prague, that never
saw pen and ink, very wittily said to a niece of King Gorboduc,
'That that is, is', so I, being Master Parson, am Master Parson;
for what is 'that' but 'that' and 'is' but 'is'?

SIR TOBY To him, Sir Topas.   15

FESTE What ho, I say! Peace in this prison!

SIR TOBY The knave counterfeits well. A good knave.

MALVOLIO (*Within*) Who calls there?

FESTE Sir Topas the curate, who comes to visit Malvolio the lunatic.

MALVOLIO Sir Topas, Sir Topas, good Sir Topas, go to my lady.   20

FESTE Out, hyperbolical fiend! How vexest thou this man! Talk'st thou
nothing but of ladies?

SIR TOBY Well said, Master Parson.

MALVOLIO Sir Topas, never was man thus wronged. Good Sir Topas,
do not think I am mad. They have laid me here in hideous darkness.   25

FESTE Fie, thou dishonest Satan! I call thee by the most modest terms,
for I am one of those gentle ones that will use the devil himself with
courtesy. Say'st thou that the house is dark?

MALVOLIO As hell, Sir Topas.

Malvolio protests that he is not mad, and that his prison is too dark. Feste (as Sir Topas) refuses to believe him and continues to torment him. Sir Toby wishes the whole business was over.

1 Tormenting Malvolio: he cannot win (in pairs)

Whatever Malvolio says, he is in a 'Catch 22' situation: he cannot win. Feste treats all his remarks as if they were made by a madman. Feste's strategy is clear: he will torment Malvolio by turning logic on its head to increase Malvolio's confusion and frustration. For example, he says that 'barricadoes' (fortifications) and 'ebony' (black wood) are 'transparent' and 'lustrous' (bright).

'The Egyptians in their fog' Feste refers to one of the plagues that Moses brought down upon Egypt, related in the Bible (Exodus, chapter 10): God caused 'thick darkness for three days'.

Pythagoras A Greek philosopher and mathematician, best known today for his theorem about right-angled triangles. But in Shakespeare's time he was famous for his doctrine of the transmigration of souls: that when a person died, his or her soul migrated to another human or animal body. This doctrine of reincarnation is rejected by Christian teaching, which believes in the resurrection of the body. As a devout puritan, Malvolio would find Pythagoras' notion very offensive.

a Take parts as Feste and Malvolio. Read lines 20–48. Feste should sound as rational as possible. Swap roles and read again. After your readings, talk together about whether you feel sympathy for Malvolio. Do you think Feste's humour is genuinely funny, or is it bitter and vicious?

b Discuss the tones of voice each character might use in a stage production of this episode.

---

clerestories windows in the upper part of a wall
constant normal
grandam grandmother
haply perhaps

allow of thy wits certify you are sane
I am for all waters I can do anything
knavery trickery
upshot finish
perdy by God (*par Dieu*)

FESTE Why, it hath bay windows transparent as barricadoes, and the   30
   clerestories toward the south-north are as lustrous as ebony; and
   yet complain'st thou of obstruction?
MALVOLIO I am not mad, Sir Topas; I say to you this house is dark.
FESTE Madman, thou errest. I say there is no darkness but ignorance,
   in which thou art more puzzled than the Egyptians in their fog.   35
MALVOLIO I say this house is as dark as ignorance, though ignorance
   were as dark as hell; and I say there was never man thus abused.
   I am no more mad than you are. Make the trial of it in any constant
   question.
FESTE What is the opinion of Pythagoras concerning wildfowl?   40
MALVOLIO That the soul of our grandam might haply inhabit a bird.
FESTE What think'st thou of his opinion?
MALVOLIO I think nobly of the soul, and no way approve his opinion.
FESTE Fare thee well. Remain thou still in darkness. Thou shalt hold
   th'opinion of Pythagoras ere I will allow of thy wits, and fear to   45
   kill a woodcock lest thou dispossess the soul of thy grandam. Fare
   thee well.
MALVOLIO Sir Topas, Sir Topas!
SIR TOBY My most exquisite Sir Topas!
FESTE Nay, I am for all waters.   50
MARIA Thou mightst have done this without thy beard and gown; he
   sees thee not.
SIR TOBY To him in thine own voice, and bring me word how thou
   find'st him. I would we were well rid of this knavery. If he may
   be conveniently delivered, I would he were, for I am now so far   55
   in offence with my niece that I cannot pursue with any safety this
   sport to the upshot. [*To Maria*] Come by and by to my chamber.
                                                    Exit [*with Maria*]
FESTE [*Sings*]   Hey Robin, jolly Robin,
                        Tell me how thy lady does.
MALVOLIO Fool!   60
FESTE [*Sings*]   My lady is unkind, perdy.
MALVOLIO Fool!
FESTE [*Sings*]   Alas, why is she so?
MALVOLIO Fool, I say!
FESTE [*Sings*]   She loves another –   65
   Who calls, ha?

Malvolio begs Feste for pen and paper to write a letter to Olivia. Feste continues to torment him by pretending to have a conversation with Sir Topas. Feste agrees to help the 'mad' Malvolio.

'Sir Topas' adds another layer to the theme of mistaken identity.

five wits (common sense, memory, judgement, imagination, fantasy)
propertied me treated me as an object, not a human being
face me out of my wits make me think I'm mad

Advise you be careful
God b'w'you God be with you
shent scolded
advantage profit
bearing delivering, carrying
counterfeit pretend

MALVOLIO Good fool, as ever thou wilt deserve well at my hand, help
me to a candle and pen, ink, and paper. As I am a gentleman, I
will live to be thankful to thee for't.

FESTE Master Malvolio?   70

MALVOLIO Ay, good fool.

FESTE Alas, sir, how fell you besides your five wits?

MALVOLIO Fool, there was never man so notoriously abused. I am as
well in my wits, fool, as thou art.

FESTE But as well? Then you are mad indeed, if you be no better in   75
your wits than a fool.

MALVOLIO They have here propertied me: keep me in darkness, send
ministers to me, asses, and do all they can to face me out of my
wits.

FESTE Advise you what you say. The minister is here. [*As Sir Topas*]   80
Malvolio, Malvolio, thy wits the heavens restore. Endeavour thyself
to sleep and leave thy vain bibble babble.

MALVOLIO Sir Topas!

FESTE [*As Sir Topas*] Maintain no words with him, good fellow. [*As
himself*] Who, I, sir? Not I, sir. God b'w'you, good Sir Topas.   85
[*As Sir Topas*] Marry, amen. [*As himself*] I will, sir, I will.

MALVOLIO Fool, fool, fool, I say!

FESTE Alas, sir, be patient. What say you, sir? I am shent for speaking
to you.

MALVOLIO Good fool, help me to some light and some paper; I tell   90
thee, I am as well in my wits as any man in Illyria.

FESTE Well-a-day, that you were, sir!

MALVOLIO By this hand, I am! Good fool, some ink, paper and light,
and convey what I will set down to my lady. It shall advantage thee
more than ever the bearing of letter did.   95

FESTE I will help you to't. But tell me true, are you not mad indeed
or do you but counterfeit?

MALVOLIO Believe me, I am not. I tell thee true.

FESTE Nay, I'll ne'er believe a madman till I see his brains. I will fetch
you light and paper and ink.   100

Malvolio promises to reward Feste who, with a song, leaves to fetch pen and paper. In Scene 3, Sebastian reflects on his good fortune. He wonders what has happened to Antonio, whose advice he needs.

---

1 Feste's song – more ridiculing of Malvolio? (in pairs)

The song may be more mockery at Malvolio's expense. As a puritan, he would be offended to think he was being helped by 'the old Vice' (see below) and the devil.

a Compose an appropriate tune for Feste's song.

b Add actions to each line as you sing or speak the song.

c Is Feste's last line ('Adieu, goodman devil') spoken to Malvolio? Or is it part of Vice's talk with the devil? Advise the actor.

2 A change of scene – but the same theme

From the darkness of Malvolio's prison, the scene changes to the sunlight of Olivia's garden. But a common theme links the two scenes: both Malvolio and Sebastian are convinced they are not mad, even though bewildering things have happened to them.

a Suggest how to manage the scene change so that the action flows swiftly between Feste's exit and Sebastian's entrance.

b Read lines 1–4 to discover how the two scenes echo each other.

3 Scene 3: a soliloquy and a proposal of marriage (in pairs)

Scene 3 presents Sebastian's wonder at what has happened: Olivia's gift to him, and Antonio's mysterious disappearance. He decides that neither he nor Olivia is mad, and willingly accepts when Olivia proposes marriage. To gain a first impression, take parts and read the whole scene. After your reading, decide whether Sebastian should speak lines 1–21 to himself, or speak some, or all of them directly to the audience.

---

requite reward
old Vice a character in medieval plays (who cut the devil's nails with a wooden dagger)
Your need to sustain to help you

lath wood
Pare cut
there he was he had been there
credit news, report

MALVOLIO Fool, I'll requite it in the highest degree. I prithee be gone.

FESTE [*Sings*]   I am gone, sir,
                 And anon, sir,
                    I'll be with you again,
                 In a trice   105
                 Like to the old Vice,
                    Your need to sustain;
                 Who, with dagger of lath,
                 In his rage and his wrath,
                    Cries, 'Ah ha' to the devil,   110
                 Like a mad lad,
                 'Pare thy nails, dad?'
                    Adieu, goodman devil.   *Exit*

Act 4 Scene 3
In Olivia's garden

Enter SEBASTIAN

SEBASTIAN This is the air, that is the glorious sun,
          This pearl she gave me, I do feel't and see't,
          And though 'tis wonder that enwraps me thus,
          Yet 'tis not madness. Where's Antonio then?
          I could not find him at the Elephant,   5
          Yet there he was, and there I found this credit,
          That he did range the town to seek me out.
          His counsel now might do me golden service,

Sebastian decides that Olivia cannot be mad, because she rules her household with total competence. Olivia arrives with a priest and proposes instant marriage. Sebastian accepts.

1 A secret marriage (in small groups)

Olivia proposes an instant marriage, but promises it will be kept secret until Sebastian is willing to make it public. Then, they will have a grand ceremony ('celebration'), suitable for her high social status ('birth'). Talk together about the following questions:

- Why does Olivia want a secret marriage?
- What's happened to her vow to mourn her brother for seven years?
- Why hasn't she called Sebastian 'Cesario' and so discovered her mistake?
- What aspects of 'appearance versus reality' are in the scene?
- Do you know of anyone who got married very quickly when he or she was abroad in a strange place?
- What does the silent priest make of it all?
- Should you just forget all the above puzzles and simply enjoy the unlikely events that Shakespeare presents?

2 Give the priest a voice

One of the questions above asked you to discuss what the priest makes of it all. Now give him a voice. Imagine he writes a sermon he will later deliver, using his experience of this episode as an example of what he wants to say. Step into role as the priest and write his account of what happened, together with the moral he thinks the events show.

3 'My most jealous and too doubtful soul'

What does line 27 add to your view of Olivia's personality?

disputes well agrees	**deceivable** misleading
instance example	**chantry by** nearby chapel
discourse reason	**Plight** pledge
wrangle argue	**Whiles** until
sway rule	**come to note** become known
dispatch carry out	**fairly note** bless

For though my soul disputes well with my sense
That this may be some error, but no madness,   10
Yet doth this accident and flood of fortune
So far exceed all instance, all discourse,
That I am ready to distrust mine eyes,
And wrangle with my reason that persuades me
To any other trust but that I am mad,   15
Or else the lady's mad; yet if 'twere so,
She could not sway her house, command her followers,
Take and give back affairs and them dispatch,
With such a smooth, discreet, and stable bearing
As I perceive she does. There's something in't   20
That is deceivable. But here the lady comes.

Enter OLIVIA *and* PRIEST

OLIVIA Blame not this haste of mine. If you mean well,
        Now go with me, and with this holy man
        Into the chantry by; there before him,
        And underneath that consecrated roof,   25
        Plight me the full assurance of your faith,
        That my most jealous and too doubtful soul
        May live at peace. He shall conceal it
        Whiles you are willing it shall come to note;
        What time we will our celebration keep   30
        According to my birth. What do you say?
SEBASTIAN I'll follow this good man, and go with you,
        And having sworn truth, ever will be true.
OLIVIA Then lead the way, good father, and heavens so shine,
        That they may fairly note this act of mine!   35

Exeunt

Looking back at Act 4
Activities for groups or individuals

1 Appearance and reality: mistaken identity

In all three scenes of Act 4, characters mistake other characters' identities. Write down who mistakes whom in each scene. Write the consequence alongside each 'mistaking'. For example, in Scene 1 Sir Andrew mistakes Sebastian for Viola-Cesario. The result is a beating.

2 Attitudes to 'madness': tormenting Malvolio

Scene 2 presents problems for a modern audience: how should they respond to the sight of Malvolio being humiliated? It seems that Elizabethans gave little thought to that question. It was an age when people were fascinated by what they called 'madness'. They visited asylums where mentally disturbed people were kept, and gained enjoyment from watching the 'mad' people. It seems likely that Shakespeare's audiences enjoyed the sight of Malvolio being treated as a madman.

Today, people with mental problems are treated much more compassionately, and the response of a modern audience is more complicated. Many feel uncomfortable about the baiting of Malvolio (pictured opposite, chained like a bear).

Write your response to Scene 2, describing what you think of how Malvolio is treated. Does he deserve what he gets?

3 Find the images

Locate each image in the script and explain what it means.

Scene 1 'I'll throw your dagger o'er the house'

Scene 2 'Out, hyperbolical fiend!'

Scene 3 'this accident and flood of fortune'

4 True lover, or . . .?

Has Sebastian fallen in love with Olivia? Or is he just taking advantage of her money and status? Think about your view of his character and try to guess at his true feelings as Olivia leads him off to marriage at the end of Act 4.

Malvolio's progress. This is how four different productions have presented Malvolio at particular moments in the play. Look back through the first four acts to identify which moment you think each picture represents. Choose suitable captions from the script.

Feste will not let Fabian see Malvolio's letter. He entertains Orsino with his word-juggling, and encourages him to hand over more money.

1 Comedian and stooges? (in groups of three)

Feste treats both Fabian and Orsino as the 'stooge' or 'straight man', the partner who feeds lines to a comedian, so that the comedian can make a witty point.

a Practise reading lines 1–38 with Feste as a kind of music-hall or double-act comedian, scoring points off his partner.

b Orsino is the most powerful person in Illyria, but Feste is almost rude to him. Try reading lines 6–38 so that Feste mocks Orsino, coming extremely close to being disrespectful to him. How does Orsino speak his lines if Feste is almost openly cheeky? Experiment with ways of showing that Orsino half suspects that he is being mocked, and becomes increasingly irritated about it.

c Experiment with other styles of speaking. Which do you think is the most appropriate tone for Feste to use?

2 Explaining the joke

Explaining a joke is a sure way to kill the humour. But two things Feste says would have made his Elizabethan audience laugh because they were well known at the time:

Line 5   Queen Elizabeth I begged a dog from a courtier, saying she would grant any request in return. He replied, 'Give me my dog again.'

Lines 16–17 A favourite joke among men of the time was that a girl's 'no, no, no, no' actually meant 'yes, yes' (try speaking the four 'no's to make them mean two 'yes's – the trick is in the emphasis). Another explanation of the joke is that negatives meant 'lips' and affirmatives meant 'mouths'. So four lips made two mouths.

---

recompense payment, exchange
trappings hangers-on, adornments
By my troth by my faith (truthfully)

double-dealing deception (or giving twice)
grace honour
flesh and blood human nature (as opposed to 'grace')

Act 5 Scene 1
In Olivia's garden

Enter FESTE and FABIAN

FABIAN Now, as thou lov'st me, let me see his letter.

FESTE Good Master Fabian, grant me another request.

FABIAN Anything.

FESTE Do not desire to see this letter.

FABIAN This is to give a dog and in recompense desire my dog again.   5

Enter DUKE [ORSINO], VIOLA, CURIO, *and Lords*

ORSINO Belong you to the Lady Olivia, friends?

FESTE Ay, sir, we are some of her trappings.

ORSINO I know thee well. How dost thou, my good fellow?

FESTE Truly, sir, the better for my foes, and the worse for my friends.

ORSINO Just the contrary: the better for thy friends.   10

FESTE No, sir, the worse.

ORSINO How can that be?

FESTE Marry, sir, they praise me, and make an ass of me. Now my foes
tell me plainly I am an ass, so that by my foes, sir, I profit in the
knowledge of myself, and by my friends I am abused; so that,   15
conclusions to be as kisses, if your four negatives make your two
affirmatives, why then, the worse for my friends and the better for
my foes.

ORSINO Why, this is excellent.

FESTE By my troth, sir, no, though it please you to be one of my friends.   20

ORSINO Thou shalt not be the worse for me; there's gold.

FESTE But that it would be double-dealing, sir, I would you could make
it another.

ORSINO O you give me ill counsel.

FESTE Put your grace in your pocket, sir, for this once, and let your   25
flesh and blood obey it.

Feste tries to persuade Orsino to give him more money, but is sent to fetch Olivia. The officers bring Antonio. He is recognised by Orsino as a past enemy, and by Viola as the one who rescued her in the duel.

1 'Lullaby to your bounty' – Feste's pun

Feste tries to beg a third coin from Orsino by counting in Latin (*'Primo, secundo, tertio'* = one, two, three), and referring to triple time ('triplex') in dance music ('measure' = dance) and the three bells of St Bennet's (a London church). Feste says he's not greedy for money, but clearly hopes that bringing Olivia will result in a further reward from Orsino. Notice how he seizes on Orsino's word 'awake' to develop an extended pun on sleeping. Suggest actions he might use with lines 35–8.

2 Report the sea-battle

Antonio obviously did great deeds in a destructive fight ('scathful grapple') against Orsino's fleet. His own ship was tiny and hardly worth capturing ('A baubling vessel . . . unprizable'). But he outfought Orsino's best ship ('most noble bottom'), and captured another with all her cargo from Crete ('the Phoenix and her fraught from Candy'). His bravery made his Illyrian enemies admire him, even though he inflicted terrible losses on them.

Write the report of the sea-battle (based on lines 40–52) from the viewpoint of one or more of the following: Antonio, Titus, Orsino, the captain of the *Phoenix* or the *Tiger*, or an ordinary seaman.

3 The voice of authority (in pairs)

Orsino is the military commander as well as the ruler of Illyria. All his previous appearances have been concerned with love, but now he takes on his official duties and speaks as a leader. Speak his lines to, and about Antonio (40–8, 58–61) in as commanding a voice as you can. Where might he vary his tone of voice?

---

triplex triple time in music
bounty generosity
covetousness ardent desire for money
Vulcan Roman god of fire, blacksmith to the gods (see p. 165)

desp'rate of shame and state recklessly disregarding disgrace and danger
distraction madness
Notable notorious
dear costly, grievous

ORSINO Well, I will be so much a sinner to be a double-dealer; there's
another.

FESTE *Primo, secundo, tertio* is a good play, and the old saying is 'The
third pays for all'; the triplex, sir, is a good tripping measure; or   30
the bells of St Bennet, sir, may put you in mind – one, two, three.

ORSINO You can fool no more money out of me at this throw. If you
will let your lady know I am here to speak with her, and bring her
along with you, it may awake my bounty further.

FESTE Marry, sir, lullaby to your bounty till I come again. I go, sir,   35
but I would not have you to think that my desire of having is the
sin of covetousness; but, as you say, sir, let your bounty take a nap.
I will awake it anon.   *Exit*

Enter ANTONIO *and* OFFICERS

VIOLA Here comes the man, sir, that did rescue me.

ORSINO That face of his I do remember well;   40
          Yet when I saw it last, it was besmeared
          As black as Vulcan, in the smoke of war.
          A baubling vessel was he captain of,
          For shallow draught and bulk unprizable,
          With which, such scathful grapple did he make   45
          With the most noble bottom of our fleet,
          That very envy, and the tongue of loss,
          Cried fame and honour on him. What's the matter?

I OFFICER Orsino, this is that Antonio
          That took the Phoenix and her fraught from Candy,   50
          And this is he that did the Tiger board,
          When your young nephew Titus lost his leg.
          Here in the streets, desp'rate of shame and state,
          In private brabble did we apprehend him.

VIOLA He did me kindness, sir, drew on my side,   55
          But in conclusion put strange speech upon me,
          I know not what 'twas, but distraction.

ORSINO Notable pirate! Thou salt-water thief!
          What foolish boldness brought thee to their mercies,
          Whom thou, in terms so bloody and so dear,   60
          Hast made thine enemies?

Antonio tells the story of how he rescued Sebastian, protected him and lent him money. Orsino dismisses the explanation as madness. Olivia arrives and, mistaking Viola for Sebastian, reproves and questions 'him'.

1 Antonio's story – act it out (in small groups)

Lines 66–81 tell the story of Antonio and Sebastian, and the 'mistaking' of Viola. As one person speaks the lines slowly, the others act out what is described. You'll find it good fun (and helpful to your understanding) if you play a speeded-up version after your first acting-out.

2 'A twenty-years' removèd thing' (in pairs)

Antonio's line 78 is a vivid image. Prepare two tableaux of the image: 'before' and 'after'. The first tableau shows warm friendship, the second shows what happens after twenty years' separation.

3 Three months or a few days?

Shakespeare seems to have forgotten what he wrote earlier in the play. Both Antonio and Orsino say that three months have passed since Viola came to court. But in Act 1 Scene 4, lines 2–3, Valentine says: 'he hath known you but three days'.

Imagine you are a teacher or lecturer. One of your students asks you if Shakespeare made a mistake. What do you reply? Page 168 will help you make your response.

4 'Now heaven walks on earth' – and a cool response

This is the first time that Orsino and Olivia meet in the play. Advise the actors how they can make the most of the stage direction: '*Enter* OLIVIA *and Attendants*', Orsino's line 86, and Olivia's lines 90–2.

---

base and ground firm reason	**int'rim** interim, time between
wrack wreckage	**vacancy** absence
beset attacked	**tended upon** served (attended)
partake share	**anon** soon
face ... acquaintance deny he knew me	**serviceable** of help

ANTONIO   Orsino, noble sir,
　　　Be pleased that I shake off these names you give me.
　　　Antonio never yet was thief or pirate,
　　　Though I confess, on base and ground enough,
　　　Orsino's enemy. A witchcraft drew me hither.   65
　　　That most ungrateful boy there by your side,
　　　From the rude sea's enraged and foamy mouth
　　　Did I redeem; a wrack past hope he was.
　　　His life I gave him, and did thereto add
　　　My love without retention, or restraint,   70
　　　All his in dedication. For his sake,
　　　Did I expose myself, pure for his love,
　　　Into the danger of this adverse town,
　　　Drew to defend him when he was beset;
　　　Where being apprehended, his false cunning   75
　　　(Not meaning to partake with me in danger)
　　　Taught him to face me out of his acquaintance,
　　　And grew a twenty-years' removèd thing
　　　While one would wink; denied me mine own purse,
　　　Which I had recommended to his use   80
　　　Not half an hour before.

VIOLA   How can this be?

ORSINO When came he to this town?

ANTONIO Today, my lord, and for three months before,
　　　No int'rim, not a minute's vacancy,
　　　Both day and night did we keep company.   85

Enter OLIVIA *and Attendants*

ORSINO Here comes the countess; now heaven walks on earth.
　　　But for thee, fellow – Fellow, thy words are madness.
　　　Three months this youth hath tended upon me,
　　　But more of that anon. Take him aside.

OLIVIA What would my lord, but that he may not have,   90
　　　Wherein Olivia may seem serviceable?
　　　Cesario, you do not keep promise with me.

VIOLA Madam!

ORSINO Gracious Olivia –

OLIVIA What do you say, Cesario? Good my lord –   95

Olivia rejects Orsino's love. He threatens to kill her, then threatens to kill Viola-Cesario, suspecting Olivia loves 'him'. Viola willingly agrees to go with Orsino. Olivia feels deceived, and sends for the Priest.

1 A strange lover: he threatens to kill! (in small groups)

Within moments of meeting Olivia, Orsino is criticising her. Even worse, he threatens to kill her! His criticism is full of religious language ('altars', 'soul', 'faithfull'st', 'devotion'). His threat to kill is made as he compares himself to Thyamus, a legendary Egyptian thief, who, surrounded by his enemies, attempted to kill the woman he loved, so that she would not fall into their hands. Use the following activities to explore lines 101–20.

a How should Orsino speak his criticism of Olivia in lines 101–4? Does he snap the lines? Or try to win her sympathy? How does he speak the four words 'What shall I do?'?

b How does Olivia reply in line 105: off-handedly? challengingly? sharply? coldly? dismissively? sympathetically ('shall become' = that brings honour to)?

c Orsino suddenly turns cruel, threatening first Olivia, then Viola-Cesario (to spite Olivia). Speak lines 106–20 as dangerous threats (meaning them), then as hopeless pleas (not meaning them). Do you think he really intends to kill either woman?

2 Love – and puzzlement!

Viola, although threatened with death, follows Orsino, declaring her love for him. Olivia feels bewildered and deceived. As you turn the page you will discover that Olivia freezes everyone into astonishment with a single word!

---

aught anything	**marble-breasted** hard-hearted
fat and fulsome gross and distasteful	**minion** favourite
ingrate ungrateful	**tender** esteem, hold, regard
unauspicious ill-omened	**jocund** gladly
savours nobly tastes honourable	**do you rest** give you comfort
cast throw aside	**feign** pretend
screws me from forces me out of	**beguiled** deceived

VIOLA My lord would speak; my duty hushes me.

OLIVIA If it be aught to the old tune, my lord,
    It is as fat and fulsome to mine ear
    As howling after music.

ORSINO   Still so cruel?

OLIVIA Still so constant, lord.   100

ORSINO What, to perverseness? You uncivil lady,
    To whose ingrate and unauspicious altars
    My soul the faithfull'st off'rings have breathed out
    That e'er devotion tendered! What shall I do?

OLIVIA Even what it please my lord that shall become him.   105

ORSINO Why should I not – had I the heart to do it –
    Like to th'Egyptian thief at point of death
    Kill what I love – a savage jealousy
    That sometimes savours nobly? But hear me this.
    Since you to non-regardance cast my faith,   110
    And that I partly know the instrument
    That screws me from my true place in your favour,
    Live you the marble-breasted tyrant still.
    But this your minion, whom I know you love,
    And whom, by heaven I swear, I tender dearly,   115
    Him will I tear out of that cruel eye
    Where he sits crownèd in his master's spite.
    Come, boy, with me; my thoughts are ripe in mischief.
    I'll sacrifice the lamb that I do love,
    To spite a raven's heart within a dove. [*Leaving*]   120

VIOLA And I most jocund, apt, and willingly,
    To do you rest, a thousand deaths would die. [*Following*]

OLIVIA Where goes Cesario?

VIOLA   After him I love
    More than I love these eyes, more than my life,
    More, by all mores, than e'er I shall love wife.   125
    If I do feign, you witnesses above
    Punish my life for tainting of my love!

OLIVIA Ay me, detested! How am I beguiled!

VIOLA Who does beguile you? Who does do you wrong?

OLIVIA Hast thou forgot thyself? Is it so long?   130
    Call forth the holy father.

                      [*Exit an Attendant*]

Olivia amazes everyone by claiming Viola-Cesario as her husband (she mistakes 'him' for Sebastian). The Priest confirms the marriage. Orsino scolds Viola-Cesario for lying, and orders 'him' away.

---

1 'Cesario, husband, stay!' – 'Husband?' (in pairs)

Olivia's command 'Cesario, husband, stay!' shocks and astonishes everyone on stage (and the audience into delight at that astonishment). Orsino's bewildered 'Husband?' increases the audience's enjoyment. It is a moment that every production wants to make as funny as possible. Take parts as Olivia and Orsino and find your own preferred way of speaking those four words.

2 Appearance versus reality? Or appearance = reality?

At line 138, Olivia challenges the play's theme of false identity: 'Be that thou know'st thou art' (admit what you truly are, namely my husband). But her appeal is full of unconscious irony. It actually reinforces the notion that things in Illyria are never what they seem. Her lines 135–9 get everything wrong even though she speaks them with conviction. Suggest how Orsino and Viola react to her appeal.

3 Step into role as the Priest (in pairs)

The Priest uses very formal language. Experiment with styles of speaking that suit his elaborate, ceremonious manner of speech.

4 A vivid image – but 'grizzle' has a different meaning

People today might interpret Orsino's harsh words to Viola-Cesario 'What wilt thou be / When time hath sowed a grizzle on thy case?' as 'What are you going to be like when you are older and discontented and grumbling (grizzly)?' But in Shakespeare's day, 'grizzle' meant 'grey hairs'.

---

baseness degrading effect
strangle thy propriety deny your
  identity (as husband)
'tis ripe the proper time
newly passed recently happened
mutual joinder both clasping

Attested vouched for
compact contract of marriage
function job as a priest
dissembling deceitful
case body, skin
trip stumble (or trap)

ORSINO   Come, away!
OLIVIA Whither, my lord? Cesario, husband, stay!
ORSINO Husband?
OLIVIA   Ay, husband. Can he that deny?
ORSINO Her husband, sirrah?
VIOLA   No, my lord, not I.
OLIVIA Alas, it is the baseness of thy fear   135
      That makes thee strangle thy propriety.
      Fear not, Cesario, take thy fortunes up;
      Be that thou know'st thou art, and then thou art
      As great as that thou fear'st.

Enter PRIEST

              O welcome, father!
      Father, I charge thee by thy reverence   140
      Here to unfold – though lately we intended
      To keep in darkness what occasion now
      Reveals before 'tis ripe – what thou dost know
      Hath newly passed between this youth and me.
PRIEST A contract of eternal bond of love,   145
      Confirmed by mutual joinder of your hands,
      Attested by the holy close of lips,
      Strengthened by th'interchangement of your rings,
      And all the ceremony of this compact
      Sealed in my function, by my testimony;   150
      Since when, my watch hath told me, toward my grave
      I have travelled but two hours.
ORSINO [*To Viola*] O thou dissembling cub! What wilt thou be
      When time hath sowed a grizzle on thy case?
      Or will not else thy craft so quickly grow   155
      That thine own trip shall be thine overthrow?
      Farewell, and take her, but direct thy feet
      Where thou and I henceforth may never meet.
VIOLA My lord, I do protest –
OLIVIA   O do not swear!
      Hold little faith, though thou hast too much fear.   160

Sir Andrew complains that Viola-Cesario has wounded him. Viola-Cesario denies it. Sir Toby enters – he has also been attacked. He scornfully dismisses Sir Andrew's offer of help.

1 Comedy, bewilderment and pathos

After the amazement of the 'husband' episode, and Orsino's vehement rejection of Viola-Cesario, Shakespeare dramatises another hilarious, bitter-sweet comic incident. Sir Andrew, beaten by Sebastian, usually performs a fearful and incredulous double-take as he catches sight of Viola and exclaims, ''Od's lifelings, here he is!'

Sir Toby's contemptuous spurning of Sir Andrew's friendship often evokes audience sympathy for the foolish knight. Take parts as Sir Andrew, Olivia, Orsino, Viola, Sir Toby and Feste and act out this episode.

- Make Sir Andrew pitiable, and his 'double-take' comic.
- Ensure that Olivia, Orsino and Viola are mystified by what they see and hear. But bring out Olivia's compassion for Sir Toby as she says 'let his hurt be looked to'.
- Sir Toby rejects Sir Andrew's offer to help him. He shows what he really thinks of Sir Andrew as he calls him 'an ass-head, and a coxcomb [conceited fool], and a knave, a thin-faced knave, a gull' (lines 190–1). Make Sir Toby's scornful dismissal as cruel as you can.
- This is the final appearance of Sir Andrew and Sir Toby. Work out how to present the stage direction '*Exeunt Feste, Fabian, Sir Toby, and Sir Andrew*' to show each man's personality. What would you hope the audience to feel about Sir Toby and Sir Andrew?
- 'Passy-measures pavin' (line 185) may mean 'drunken slowcoach' (Sir Toby drunkenly slurs 'passing measure pavane': a slow and stately dance). But no one is certain of the meaning. Make up your own suggestion of what is in Sir Toby's mind.

---

presently immediately
bloody coxcomb bleeding head
incardinate incarnate (in the flesh)
'Od's lifelings by God's life
bespake you fair spoke kindly to you
halting limping

othergates in another way, otherwise
Sot drunkard (or fool)
his eyes were set blind drunk
dressed bandaged
gull fool, dupe

Enter SIR ANDREW [*his head bleeding*]

SIR ANDREW For the love of God, a surgeon! Send one presently to
Sir Toby.

OLIVIA What's the matter?

SIR ANDREW H'as broke my head across, and has given Sir Toby a
bloody coxcomb, too. For the love of God, your help! I had rather   165
than forty pound I were at home.

OLIVIA Who has done this, Sir Andrew?

SIR ANDREW The count's gentleman, one Cesario. We took him for a
coward, but he's the very devil incardinate.

ORSINO My gentleman Cesario?   170

SIR ANDREW 'Od's lifelings, here he is! You broke my head for nothing,
and that that I did, I was set on to do't by Sir Toby.

VIOLA Why do you speak to me? I never hurt you.
    You drew your sword upon me without cause,
    But I bespake you fair, and hurt you not.   175

Enter [SIR] TOBY *and* CLOWN [FESTE]

SIR ANDREW If a bloody coxcomb be a hurt, you have hurt me; I think
you set nothing by a bloody coxcomb. Here comes Sir Toby
halting – you shall hear more; but if he had not been in drink, he
would have tickled you othergates than he did.

ORSINO How now, gentleman? How is't with you?   180

SIR TOBY That's all one. H'as hurt me, and there's th'end on't. Sot,
didst see Dick Surgeon, sot?

FESTE O he's drunk, Sir Toby, an hour agone; his eyes were set at eight
i'th'morning.

SIR TOBY Then he's a rogue, and a passy-measures pavin. I hate a   185
drunken rogue.

OLIVIA Away with him! Who hath made this havoc with them?

SIR ANDREW I'll help you, Sir Toby, because we'll be dressed
together.

SIR TOBY Will you help – an ass-head, and a coxcomb, and a knave,   190
a thin-faced knave, a gull?

OLIVIA Get him to bed, and let his hurt be looked to.
                                [Exeunt Feste, Fabian, Sir Toby, and Sir Andrew]

Sebastian's appearance amazes everyone. Antonio expresses everyone's thoughts on seeing a double vision. The twins question each other and begin to find out that they are indeed related.

Shakespeare now provides yet another comic episode that becomes charged with hope. Everyone is once more amazed, this time by the entrance of someone who is the double of Viola-Cesario. How can one person be in two places at once? Antonio voices what everyone is thinking: 'An apple cleft in two is not more twin'. No one believes the evidence of their own eyes. Orsino calls it 'A natural perspective' (a distorting mirror which makes one image into two). And Olivia's exclamation as she sees she has two husbands causes audience laughter: 'Most wonderful!' The mood becomes poignant as each twin begins to realise that the other has survived the shipwreck.

An activity on page 150 invites you to compile an assignment on the brother and sister twins.

strange regard odd look	**Of charity** tell me (out of kindness)
but so late ago not long ago	**suited** dressed like that
habit costume	**in that dimension . . . participate** still
racked pained	the same person as I was born
deity divinity (like God, everywhere at	**as the rest goes even** as everything
the same time)	else suggests

Enter SEBASTIAN

SEBASTIAN I am sorry, madam, I have hurt your kinsman.
　　　　But had it been the brother of my blood,
　　　　I must have done no less with wit and safety.　　　　195
　　　　You throw a strange regard upon me, and by that
　　　　I do perceive it hath offended you.
　　　　Pardon me, sweet one, even for the vows
　　　　We made each other but so late ago.
ORSINO One face, one voice, one habit, and two persons –　　　200
　　　　A natural perspective, that is and is not!
SEBASTIAN Antonio! O my dear Antonio,
　　　　How have the hours racked and tortured me,
　　　　Since I have lost thee!
ANTONIO Sebastian are you?
SEBASTIAN　　　　　　　　Fear'st thou that, Antonio?　　　205
ANTONIO How have you made division of yourself?
　　　　An apple cleft in two is not more twin
　　　　Than these two creatures. Which is Sebastian?
OLIVIA Most wonderful!
SEBASTIAN Do I stand there? I never had a brother;　　　210
　　　　Nor can there be that deity in my nature
　　　　Of here and everywhere. I had a sister,
　　　　Whom the blind waves and surges have devoured.
　　　　Of charity, what kin are you to me?
　　　　What countryman? What name? What parentage?　　　215
VIOLA Of Messaline. Sebastian was my father;
　　　　Such a Sebastian was my brother, too;
　　　　So went he suited to his wat'ry tomb.
　　　　If spirits can assume both form and suit,
　　　　You come to fright us.
SEBASTIAN　　　　　　　　A spirit I am indeed,　　　220
　　　　But am in that dimension grossly clad
　　　　Which from the womb I did participate.
　　　　Were you a woman – as the rest goes even –
　　　　I should my tears let fall upon your cheek,
　　　　And say, 'Thrice welcome, drownèd Viola.'　　　225

All is revealed! Sebastian and Viola are reunited. Viola tells of her disguise. Orsino hints at marriage to Viola. She confirms that she loves him and then reports that Malvolio has had the Captain arrested.

1 Uncertainty – hope – joy! (in pairs)

The twins' reunion, as they move from hope to certainty that the other lives, is a moving episode. Take parts as Sebastian and Viola and speak lines 210–42. Try to express their initial puzzlement, then growing hope, as they exchange details of their father, and their final joy as they each realise they really have found their lost sibling. After your reading, make notes on how each moment in the exchange could be played, giving reasons. For example, why do you think Viola forbids an embrace at line 235?

2 Nature sorts things out! A bowling image

Sebastian tells Olivia that she could have been engaged to a woman, 'But nature to her bias drew in that' (line 244). The image is from the game of bowls. Because each bowl has a lead weight (a bias) inside, it does not run straight, but runs towards its target along an indirect, curved route. So Sebastian suggests that eventually, if indirectly, nature sorts out muddles and mistakes as it follows its course. Suggest an action that Sebastian could perform as he speaks line 244, to make his meaning clear to the audience.

3 Orsino's love abruptly changes – is he a true lover?

Orsino suddenly switches his love from Olivia to Viola (line 250) when he discovers that his handsome page is really a woman. As director of the play, would you want to make the audience laugh at this sudden switch of affection? Write a paragraph giving your own reaction to what Orsino says.

---

lets   hinders, interferes
usurped   falsely taken
cohere and jump   concur and agree
maiden weeds   women's clothes
occurrence of my fortune
 happenings of my life
contracted   betrothed, engaged

glass   mirror (the perspective of line
 201 is truthful)
happy wreck   fortunate accident
orbèd . . . night   sun (see p. 164)
action   lawsuit
in durance   imprisoned
suit   legal action

VIOLA My father had a mole upon his brow.

SEBASTIAN And so had mine.

VIOLA And died that day when Viola from her birth
　　　　Had numbered thirteen years.

SEBASTIAN O that record is lively in my soul!　　　　　　　　230
　　　　He finishèd indeed his mortal act
　　　　That day that made my sister thirteen years.

VIOLA If nothing lets to make us happy both,
　　　　But this my masculine usurped attire,
　　　　Do not embrace me, till each circumstance,　　　　235
　　　　Of place, time, fortune, do cohere and jump
　　　　That I am Viola, which to confirm
　　　　I'll bring you to a captain in this town,
　　　　Where lie my maiden weeds; by whose gentle help
　　　　I was preserved – to serve this noble count.　　　　240
　　　　All the occurrence of my fortune since
　　　　Hath been between this lady and this lord.

SEBASTIAN [To Olivia] So comes it, lady, you have been mistook.
　　　　But nature to her bias drew in that.
　　　　You would have been contracted to a maid;　　　　245
　　　　Nor are you therein, by my life, deceived;
　　　　You are betrothed both to a maid and man.

ORSINO Be not amazed, right noble is his blood.
　　　　If this be so – as yet the glass seems true –
　　　　I shall have share in this most happy wreck.　　　　250
　　　　[To Viola] Boy, thou hast said to me a thousand times
　　　　Thou never shouldst love woman like to me.

VIOLA And all those sayings will I overswear,
　　　　And all those swearings keep as true in soul
　　　　As doth that orbèd continent the fire　　　　255
　　　　That severs day from night.

ORSINO　　　　　　　　　　　　　　　　Give me thy hand.
　　　　And let me see thee in thy woman's weeds.

VIOLA The captain that did bring me first on shore
　　　　Hath my maid's garments; he upon some action
　　　　Is now in durance, at Malvolio's suit,　　　　260
　　　　A gentleman and follower of my lady's.

Feste brings Malvolio's letter. It reports Malvolio's suffering and his indignation. Olivia orders Malvolio to be brought in. She proposes a joint wedding celebration for the two couples at her house.

---

1 Feste's revenge? (in pairs)

a Feste has not bothered to deliver Malvolio's letter as promptly as he could. It seems he is deliberately prolonging Malvolio's suffering and humiliation. Tell each other what you feel this delay suggests about Feste.

b Feste uses a striking image to describe Malvolio, 'he holds Belzebub at the stave's end': Malvolio is fighting to keep the devil at a distance (as if with a long staff or rod). With your partner, construct a tableau to show the image.

2 Reading the letter – three styles (in threes)

Olivia won't allow Feste to read Malvolio's letter, because he puts on a mad voice. But how does Fabian read it, and how would Malvolio speak what he's written? Read lines 282–90:

- as Feste
- as Fabian
- as Malvolio.

What does the letter tell you about Malvolio's state of mind?

3 Does handwriting reveal personality?

Some people believe that handwriting reveals character – do you? Write out Malvolio's letter (lines 282–90) in a style of handwriting which you think reflects his personality.

---

enlarge   release
much distract   mad
most extracting frenzy   madness
epistles/gospels   letters/truths (and puns on religious meanings, see p. 167)
skills not much   doesn't matter
well edified   satisfied
vox   voice (Latin), style of speaking

perpend   consider, pay attention
induced   persuaded
semblance   appearance
leave my duty . . . unthought of   go beyond my place as steward
crown th'alliance on't   celebrate the double marriage
at my proper cost   I'll pay all expenses

OLIVIA He shall enlarge him; fetch Malvolio hither.
>   And yet, alas, now I remember me,
>   They say, poor gentleman, he's much distract.

Enter CLOWN [FESTE], *with a letter, and* FABIAN

>   A most extracting frenzy of mine own   265
>   From my remembrance clearly banished his.
>   How does he, sirrah?

FESTE Truly, madam, he holds Belzebub at the stave's end as well as
a man in his case may do; h'as here writ a letter to you; I should
have given't you today morning. But as a madman's epistles are no   270
gospels, so it skills not much when they are delivered.

OLIVIA Open't and read it.

FESTE Look then to be well edified when the fool delivers the madman.
[*Reads madly*] 'By the Lord, madam –'

OLIVIA How now, art thou mad?   275

FESTE No, madam, I do but read madness; and your ladyship will have
it as it ought to be, you must allow *vox*.

OLIVIA Prithee read i'thy right wits.

FESTE So I do, madonna; but to read his right wits is to read thus.
Therefore, perpend, my princess, and give ear.   280

OLIVIA [*To Fabian*] Read it you, sirrah.

FABIAN [*Reads*] 'By the Lord, madam, you wrong me, and the world
shall know it. Though you have put me into darkness, and given
your drunken cousin rule over me, yet have I the benefit of my
senses as well as your ladyship. I have your own letter that induced   285
me to the semblance I put on; with the which I doubt not but to
do myself much right, or you much shame. Think of me as you
please. I leave my duty a little unthought of and speak out of my
injury.

>   The madly used Malvolio.'   290

OLIVIA Did he write this?

FESTE Ay, madam.

ORSINO This savours not much of distraction.

OLIVIA See him delivered, Fabian; bring him hither.

>   [*Exit Fabian*]

>   My lord, so please you, these things further thought on,   295
>   To think me as well a sister as a wife,
>   One day shall crown th'alliance on't, so please you,
>   Here at my house, and at my proper cost.

Orsino proposes marriage to Viola. Malvolio shows Olivia the forged letter, describes what has happened to him, and demands an explanation. Olivia recognises that the letter is in Maria's handwriting.

1 'You are she!' Can she tell them apart? (in small groups)

In some productions, Olivia has looked away from the twins and now, at line 305, cannot tell which is Viola. Do you think Olivia has difficulty recognising which is Viola and which is Sebastian? Take sides and argue for and against. But the answer best lies in what happens in performance. So act out different versions of what happens as Olivia speaks 'Ah, sister, you are she!' Which interpretation do you think is most appropriate to the mood of the scene?

2 Malvolio: appearance and speaking style (in pairs)

In performance, Malvolio often appears bedraggled and dirt-stained, his clothes in rags and his cross-garters all unwound. Once he appeared in a strait-jacket. Think about how you would stage his appearance and his manner of speaking. Would you want him to win the audience's sympathy for his mistreatment? Again, the best way of deciding is in performance – but don't tear your clothes! Try out different ways of entering and speaking lines 309–23. Speak very angrily; then in a very calm, dignified and reasoned style; and then as if you are close to tears. Finally, speak the lines as if you were utterly bewildered.

3 Should Malvolio glare at the Priest?

In one production, Malvolio glared at the Priest with great indignation as he spoke line 321. Give reasons why you think such a piece of stage business is appropriate or not.

apt ready	**invention** (line 312) style
quits releases	**lighter people** servants
mettle nature	**geck and gull** fool and dupe
peruse read	**invention** (line 323) trick, deceit
Write from it write differently	**the character** my handwriting

144

ORSINO Madam, I am most apt t'embrace your offer.
　　　　[*To Viola*] Your master quits you; and for your service
　　　　　　done him,　　　　　　　　　　　　　　　　　　　　300
　　　　So much against the mettle of your sex,
　　　　So far beneath your soft and tender breeding,
　　　　And since you called me master for so long,
　　　　Here is my hand; you shall from this time be
　　　　Your master's mistress.
OLIVIA　　　　　　　　　　　　Ah, sister, you are she!　　　305

　　　　　　Enter [FABIAN *with*] MALVOLIO

ORSINO Is this the madman?
OLIVIA　　　　　　　　　　Ay, my lord, this same.
　　　　How now, Malvolio?
MALVOLIO　　　　　　　　　Madam, you have done me wrong,
　　　　Notorious wrong.
OLIVIA　　　　　　　Have I, Malvolio? No.
MALVOLIO Lady, you have. Pray you, peruse that letter.
　　　　You must not now deny it is your hand;　　　　　310
　　　　Write from it, if you can, in hand, or phrase,
　　　　Or say 'tis not your seal, not your invention.
　　　　You can say none of this. Well, grant it then,
　　　　And tell me, in the modesty of honour,
　　　　Why you have given me such clear lights of favour,　　315
　　　　Bade me come smiling and cross-gartered to you,
　　　　To put on yellow stockings, and to frown
　　　　Upon Sir Toby, and the lighter people;
　　　　And acting this in an obedient hope,
　　　　Why have you suffered me to be imprisoned,　　　320
　　　　Kept in a dark house, visited by the priest,
　　　　And made the most notorious geck and gull,
　　　　That e'er invention played on? Tell me, why?
OLIVIA Alas, Malvolio, this is not my writing,
　　　　Though I confess much like the character.　　　　325
　　　　But, out of question, 'tis Maria's hand.
　　　　And now I do bethink me, it was she
　　　　First told me thou wast mad; then cam'st in smiling,
　　　　And in such forms which here were presupposed
　　　　Upon thee in the letter. Prithee, be content;　　　330

Fabian reveals the plot against Malvolio and tells that Sir Toby has married Maria. Feste teases Malvolio, who leaves, swearing revenge. Orsino looks forward to his marriage to Viola.

1 Malvolio's revenge

'I'll be revenged on the whole pack of you!' (line 355). Does Malvolio mean it – and does he get his revenge? Some people think that the line is a forewarning of the English Civil War, which took place forty years after *Twelfth Night* was written. The Puritans seized power, closed the theatres, and attempted to end all frivolity and merrymaking.

a Write a short story or poem called 'Malvolio's revenge'.

b Decide how Malvolio speaks line 355: angrily? in tears? in a whisper? Also decide how everyone reacts – and how Malvolio leaves.

c Write a paragraph telling how, in your production, you hope the audience will feel about Malvolio at this moment.

2 Olivia's final line – anger or sympathy?

In one production, Olivia was clearly very angry with Feste. She hit him as she spoke line 356. Is such an action in character with Olivia, and appropriate to the final moments of the play? Suggest what you would advise Olivia to do at line 356.

3 Creating a mood for (almost) the final moment

Everyone except Feste leaves the stage at line 365. Imagine you are directing the play. What atmosphere do you wish to create for the audience in these closing moments? A mood of harmony, with the characters pairing up happily as they leave? Or some other atmosphere? Write notes on how you would direct the characters to leave the stage to establish the mood you wish to create. Don't forget Antonio, who has been a silent watcher for so long.

---

practice trick
shrewdly passed mischievously worked
grounds reasons
plaintiff accuser
Taint poison, contaminate

Upon some stubborn . . . him because we thought him stiff-necked and uncivil
importance insistence
whirligig roundabout, whip top
convents calls us together
combination union, marriage

This practice hath most shrewdly passed upon thee;
But when we know the grounds, and authors of it,
Thou shalt be both the plaintiff and the judge
Of thine own cause.

FABIAN   Good madam, hear me speak,
And let no quarrel, nor no brawl to come,   335
Taint the condition of this present hour,
Which I have wondered at. In hope it shall not,
Most freely I confess, myself and Toby
Set this device against Malvolio here,
Upon some stubborn and uncourteous parts   340
We had conceived against him. Maria writ
The letter, at Sir Toby's great importance,
In recompense whereof he hath married her.
How with a sportful malice it was followed
May rather pluck on laughter than revenge,   345
If that the injuries be justly weighed,
That have on both sides passed.

OLIVIA Alas, poor fool, how have they baffled thee!

FESTE Why, 'Some are born great, some achieve greatness, and some
have greatness thrown upon them.' I was one, sir, in this interlude,   350
one Sir Topas, sir – but that's all one. 'By the Lord, fool, I am not
mad.' But do you remember – 'Madam, why laugh you at such a
barren rascal, and you smile not, he's gagged'? And thus the
whirligig of time brings in his revenges.

MALVOLIO I'll be revenged on the whole pack of you!   [*Exit*]   355

OLIVIA He hath been most notoriously abused.

ORSINO Pursue him, and entreat him to a peace.
He hath not told us of the captain yet.

                                              [*Exit Fabian*]

When that is known, and golden time convents,
A solemn combination shall be made   360
Of our dear souls. Meantime, sweet sister,
We will not part from hence. Cesario, come –
For so you shall be while you are a man,
But when in other habits you are seen,
Orsino's mistress, and his fancy's queen.   365

                                    Exeunt [*all but Feste*]

Feste, alone on stage, sings about growing up, about being tolerated in childhood, rejected in adulthood, unsuccessful in marriage, and drunk in old age. But nothing really matters; the actors will always try to please.

Feste's haunting song closes the play. Learn the song and sing or speak it, individually or chorally, to bring out its mysterious quality (see p. 151).

foolish thing child
toy trifle, triviality
man's estate manhood

swaggering blustering
tosspots drunkards

(*Clown sings*)

When that I was and-a little tiny boy,
  With hey, ho, the wind and the rain,
A foolish thing was but a toy,
  For the rain it raineth every day.

But when I came to man's estate,   370
  With hey, ho, the wind and the rain,
'Gainst knaves and thieves men shut their gate,
  For the rain it raineth every day.

But when I came, alas, to wive,
  With hey, ho, the wind and the rain,   375
By swaggering could I never thrive,
  For the rain it raineth every day.

But when I came unto my beds,
  With hey, ho, the wind and the rain,
With tosspots still 'had drunken heads,   380
  For the rain it raineth every day.

A great while ago the world begun,
  With hey, ho, the wind and the rain,
But that's all one, our play is done,
  And we'll strive to please you every day.   [*Exit*]   385

Looking back at the play
Activities for groups or individuals

'What kin are you to me?' Sebastian and Viola marvel that the other is alive. How closely should the actors playing Viola and Sebastian resemble each other? Does it matter if they are not 'identical'? Use this picture and those on pages v, xii and 138 to help you compile an assignment on 'The twins in *Twelfth Night*'. It can include costume designs, notes and drawings of hairstyles and mannerisms the twins might share, and an analysis of the dramatic effects caused by the separation and reunion of the twins.

1 Feste's final song

On stage, the mood of Feste's final song is often sad and regretful. But when the play was performed in Shakespeare's own lifetime, Feste probably danced a jig (a merry dance) and sang in a lively, cheerful manner. Feste's mysterious song has been interpreted in very different ways. Which of the following descriptions do you think is the most appropriate? See picture caption, page 148.

moving, poignant and uneven   'sardonic and satirical'
'meant as a cheerful conclusion'   'melancholy beauty'
'clumsy and tacked on'   'haunting refrain'
'less cheerful than might be expected'   'disturbing'

What mood would you wish to create with these final words? Talk together about how you would stage the song. Act out your version.

2 *Twelfth Night*: a website

Work in a group. Design a website for the play. Pool ideas to decide what to include (e.g. illustrations, graphics, quotations, character studies).

3 Illustrations – your preferences

Look through all the photographs in this edition. Select the five you like best. Write a paragraph on each saying why you enjoy it.

4 Show the relationships of the characters

Turn to page 1 and redesign it as your own cast list. Make the relationships of the characters as clear as possible.

5 Make your own video of a scene from *Twelfth Night*

Choose a scene or incident. Find a space in the school or college grounds, learn your lines, rehearse your scene – and shoot it!

6 A comedy that ends uncertainly?

In traditional productions, the play ended in harmony. Illusions were finally banished, and happy times lay ahead, even for Sir Andrew and Sir Toby. Malvolio's threat of revenge struck the only harsh note. Modern productions sometimes show less harmonious endings. Use your knowledge of the whole play to write an extended essay on '*Twelfth Night*: a comedy that ends in uncertainty'.

What is the play about?

Imagine that you can travel back in time to around 1600. You meet William Shakespeare a few minutes after he has finished writing *Twelfth Night*, just before he takes it into rehearsal with his company, The King's Men. You ask him, 'What is the play about?'

Perhaps Shakespeare would reply, 'Think about the title, *Twelfth Night*. You can take it as a story about the merry-making that happens for the twelve days after Christmas. Everything is about celebration, eating, drinking and enjoyment. But after Twelfth Night the carnival atmosphere ends, and it's back to the normal world.'

But nobody really knows how Shakespeare might reply. Like most great artists, Shakespeare does not seem interested in explaining his work, but leaves it up to others. He just says, 'Here it is. Read it, perform it, make of it what you will.' And indeed, *What You Will* is the subtitle of the play. Since *Twelfth Night* was first performed, plenty of people have accepted that invitation to make their own interpretation of it. The following pages give some of those different readings. They show that the play can be approached, explained and performed in many ways, all of which have a claim to being 'true'.

First, you could think of *Twelfth Night* as the dramatisation of a story. A pair of twins are shipwrecked and land separately on the coast of Illyria. Each thinks the other is drowned. The sister, Viola, disguises herself as a boy, enters the service of a nobleman, Duke Orsino, and is sent by him to carry messages of love to the countess Olivia. A foolish knight, Sir Andrew Aguecheek, also hopes to win Olivia. But she takes no notice of Sir Andrew, rejects Orsino, and falls in love with the disguised Viola!

The result is all kinds of confusions, watched sardonically by the fool, Feste. In a parallel plot, Olivia's puritan steward Malvolio is tricked into thinking that she loves him. He is humiliated and mistreated for that delusion, mainly by Olivia's drunken uncle, Sir Toby Belch, and Feste. Eventually all ends happily for most characters. Viola is reunited with her twin brother Sebastian, and marriages are planned. But Sir Andrew Aguecheek gets a beating, and Malvolio ends the play angry and threatening revenge.

Or you could think of *Twelfth Night* as a particular type of play. For example, you might approach it as simply a comedy, a very amusing and charming play, sunny and always enjoyable. Filled with innocent laughter and preposterous situations, it has a happy ending which restores harmony to the temporary confusion of Illyria. All the characters are likeable and funny, Sir Toby is a lovable rogue, and even Malvolio has his comic appeal, especially when he gets what he deserves at the play's end. In this view, the play is simply a delightful entertainment which must never be taken seriously.

Alternatively you could take the approach that *Twelfth Night* is a poignant, elegiac play, sentimental and wistful. The humour, apart from Sir Toby's coarseness, is witty and tender. There are many moving moments as Viola speaks her beautiful and poignant lines of love. She longs for a fulfilment which, until the end of the play, is out of her grasp. An elegiac note is struck constantly by the many references to time ('The clock upbraids me with the waste of time'), and is heard in the sound of the ever-changing sea echoing through the play. Feste's songs are reminders that love, like life, will end. The play is a plea for a quiet acceptance of the inevitable, and for finding solace in whatever temporary happiness we can grasp.

A different approach again would be to think of the play as a comedy with troubling undertones. Here, it is regarded as an upsetting play which seems light and amusing on the surface, but has dark and harsh depths. It is an uneasy play about outsiders who lose. Antonio is left sad and alone at the end. Malvolio leaves seeking revenge, not reconciliation. Orsino and Olivia are seen as smug and self-centred. They learn little or nothing, and are just the same at the play's end as at the beginning.

Illyria is an oppressive society where no one at the top works. It breeds self-indulgence in idle aristocrats. Sir Toby and his fellow-conspirators are prompted by ill-will towards Malvolio. The cruel baiting of Malvolio is little more than theatre as blood sport. Malvolio is a scapegoat, because Illyria needs him as someone to punish for the misdeeds of society. The play is a cruel satire which foreshadows Shakespeare's tragedies. It forecasts the English Civil War, which will see the triumph of the Puritans and the extinguishing of theatre and merriment.

One way of answering the question 'What is *Twelfth Night* about?' is to identify the themes of the play. These include love, appearance versus reality, acting and theatre, madness, and time.

Love

The play is about love in its many forms, but with true love winning through at the end. The very first line announces that love will be a central theme: 'If music be the food of love, play on'.

Twelfth Night presents a rich variety of types of love. Olivia and Orsino are the mourning lady and romantic hero of literary convention. Their self-centred love is transformed to genuine love by the constancy and integrity of Viola, the embodiment of true and faithful love. Even Sir Toby finds love of a sort with Maria. Sir Andrew and Malvolio learn that playing at love, or self-love, is not enough.

The modern, western idea is that individuals fall in love and marry simply by choice. In Elizabethan England, that belief was not held by everyone. Among the nobility and rich families, marriages were often arranged for the purpose of extending or maintaining wealth, land and power. Personal choice was less important. The economic reality of arranged marriages was overlaid by two beliefs revealed in stories and plays:

Courtly love   Women were 'put on a pedestal' and worshipped from afar as unattainable goddesses (just as Orsino loves Olivia). Only by long devotion, trials and suffering, could a man win his ideal woman, the 'fair, cruel maid' of literature. Such love was sexless and idealised. In reality, it usually meant that men like Orsino were in love with the idea of love itself.

Romantic love   This was also idealised and unsexual, but it included 'love at first sight', with marriage as its result. Viola, even though she is level-headed and clear-sighted, falls head over heels in love with the self-indulgent Orsino. Olivia is similarly entranced by her first sight of Viola disguised as Cesario.

Both kinds of love produced 'the melancholy lover', the man who suffers for his love. Orsino fits the type as he sighs and fantasises about Olivia.

Shakespeare drew heavily upon these conventions of love. His genius lay in being able to mock the conventions and to suggest that love could be a partnership of equals. He saw that women's desires and capacity for feeling were on equal terms with men's, not inferior to them.

Love – and appearance versus reality. Two major themes of *Twelfth Night* are combined as Olivia (right) declares her love for the disguised Viola (in this production she posed as a shipwrecked cabinboy). Compare this picture with those on pages vii and 78 showing how the same moment was staged in different productions. Write notes on your responses to these portrayals.

Appearance versus reality

Nothing is as it seems in *Twelfth Night*. A concern with the difference between appearance and reality runs all through the play, most notably in Viola's disguise as a boy, Cesario, and Malvolio's self-delusion that he is loved by Olivia.

Characters constantly mistake each other. Olivia falls for Viola-Cesario, thinking 'he' is a young man. Malvolio mistakes the forged letter as a true declaration of Olivia's love for him. His 'mistaking' is at first ludicrous and funny, but then develops into cruel baiting and humiliation.

Viola and Sir Andrew are both tricked into thinking the other is a superb swordsman; a farcical duel is the outcome. Antonio defends Viola, thinking her to be Sebastian. He becomes bitter when Viola denies she knows him and does not return the money he lent to Sebastian. Orsino also turns against her when he mistakenly thinks his faithful page Cesario has betrayed him and married Olivia.

Because Sebastian is Viola's twin, he is constantly mistaken for her/'him'. Sir Toby and Sir Andrew get their heads bloodied for their mistake, but Olivia's mistake results in her gaining a husband.

The play delights in double-dealing, wordplay and illusion. Just as relationships between characters are unstable, so too are the meanings of words. Feste always puns and riddles, and sees himself as Olivia's 'corrupter of words' (see p. 70).

This recurring theme of appearance versus reality gives actors many opportunities to exploit the dramatic irony which arises from disguise and mistaken identity. It also enables them to entertain audiences by showing just how slippery language can be.

Acting and theatre

Twelfth Night revels in its own theatricality. The most telling example is just after Malvolio's appearance in yellow stockings, cross-gartered and smiling. Taunted by Sir Toby, Malvolio stalks off, confident Olivia loves him. Fabian speaks a daringly theatrical line: 'If this were played upon a stage now, I would condemn it as an improbable fiction.' The fact that it *is* being played on a stage, and *is* an improbable fiction always produces audience laughter.

Theatrical words recur: 'speech', 'part', 'con' (learn a part), 'play'. The many examples of **dramatic irony** also display the play's interest in the theatre. Dramatic irony is present when the audience knows something which a character on stage does not. When Viola says 'I am not what I am', Olivia is unaware of the full significance of Viola's words, whereas Viola and the audience realise what is really meant: that Viola is female. The emphasis on disguise in *Twelfth Night* means that the play is full of dramatic irony – a source of great amusement!

Madness

Madness, in different forms, runs through the play. Most obvious is the tormenting of Malvolio. Sir Toby treats Malvolio as if he has been driven mad by love, and has locked him in a dark room. Feste, posing as Sir Topas, tries to convince Malvolio that he is indeed mad. Malvolio's ill-treatment reflects the Elizabethan belief that 'mad' people were possessed by devils, and should be confined in a dark place (see p. 94).

Twelfth Night portrays other examples of the madness of love. Orsino, threatening to kill both Olivia and Viola in the final scene, is momentarily mentally unbalanced. Olivia has been told that Malvolio is 'tainted in's wits'. Passionately waiting for Viola-Cesario to arrive, she exclaims 'I am as mad as he / If sad and merry madness equal be' (Act 3 Scene 4, lines 14–15). Sebastian, filled with 'wonder' because Olivia has fallen in love with him, rejects ideas of madness, unwilling to believe that 'I am mad, / Or else the lady's mad' (Act 4 Scene 3, lines 15–16).

Time

A sense of time pervades the play. The shipwrecked Viola decides to go to Orsino's court, but leaves what may result to time: 'What else may hap, to time I will commit' (Act 1 Scene 2, line 60). Disguised as Cesario, she realises that Olivia has fallen in love with her, and exclaims, 'O time, thou must untangle this, not I' (Act 2 Scene 2, line 37).

Viola willingly accepts that time will work things out, but in a later exchange with Orsino she comments on the destructive effects of time. Orsino reflects on the brevity of women's beauty, 'For women are as roses, whose fair flower, / Being once displayed, doth fall that very hour', and Viola agrees, 'To die, even when they to perfection grow!' (Act 2 Scene 4, lines 36–7, 39). That notion of time's inevitable progress is also evident in Olivia's remark that 'The clock upbraids me with the waste of time' (Act 3 Scene 1, line 115). Most famously, Feste taunts Malvolio at the play's end with 'And thus the whirligig of time brings in his revenges.'

◆ Imagine that you are asked to explain what *Twelfth Night* is about by a six-year-old child, by a student of your own age, and by your teacher or lecturer. Write your reply to each, using pages 152–7 to help you.

Characters

Viola

Viola represents a contrast to other major characters who are deceived by appearances. Unlike them she is not in the grip of illusion. Her dramatic function is to lead Olivia and Orsino out of their fantasies about love and help them realise what true love can really be.

Virtually all interpretations agree that Viola represents true love in the play. She is not self-seeking, but self-sacrificing. She speaks simply and directly about her love in language which is not affected, but sincere. Her love for Orsino is constant, deep and pure. The following list summarises what often appears in character descriptions of Viola – that she:

- remains true to Orsino throughout the play
- unquestioningly carries out Orsino's orders to woo Olivia
- speaks the most moving and sincere lines about love in the play
- tells Olivia what genuine love really is like
- is not interested in status, but in individuals
- is willing to die for love when Orsino threatens her
- by the example of her love, ensures that Olivia and Orsino turn away from self-indulgent and self-deceiving love.

The plot device of disguise enables Shakespeare to suggest that Viola is a more complex character than might appear at first sight. As the above list shows, she woos another woman on behalf of the man she loves and, like Olivia, she falls quickly in love. Audiences are often puzzled by just what she sees in the evidently self-centred, posturing Orsino, a man who does not know what true love is. Her love seems to make her blind to the less attractive side of his nature. Is she, too, deceived by appearances? And for all her clear-sightedness, in one episode of the play she is fooled into thinking that Sir Andrew Aguecheek is a formidable duellist ('a devil in private brawl'), although her duping may be merely a device to fulfil the demands of the comic plot.

- On her first appearance in Act 1 Scene 2, why does Viola say about Orsino 'He was a bachelor then'?
- What does Viola see in Orsino?
- Study the picture opposite and compare it with the picture on page vi. What do you think is going through Viola's mind at this moment?

Orsino

Orsino is Shakespeare's presentation of 'the melancholy lover', in love with the idea of love itself, and unable to distinguish between appearance and reality. Look at the picture below and that on page vi and use the following statements to write a character study of Orsino.

- He is changeable and moody ('Enough; no more').
- He wallows in his emotions ('Love-thoughts lie rich').
- He talks incessantly of love ('O spirit of love').
- He thinks his love greater than anyone else's ('my love, more noble than the world').
- He considers himself an authority on love ('such as I am, all true lovers are').
- He speaks the language of exaggeration ('Give me excess of it', 'as hungry as the sea').
- He links love with sickness ('sicken and so die').
- He thinks Olivia will totally submit to his love ('one selfsame king').
- He worships Olivia like a goddess ('now heaven walks on earth').
- He does not woo Olivia himself, but sends messengers.
- He threatens to murder Viola-Cesario.
- He switches his love abruptly from Olivia to Viola.
- His last words ('his fancy's queen') do not suggest true love, but romantic fantasy – he substitutes one dream for another.

Olivia

Olivia has vowed to shut herself away from the world for seven years in mourning for her dead brother. She speedily breaks that vow. Like Orsino, Olivia confuses illusion with reality. Misled by outward appearances, she mistakes infatuation for love, as does Orsino, and her love proves similarly self-deceiving and sentimental. In particular, Olivia:

- thinks highly of her own good looks ('Is't not well done?')
- is quickly infatuated by Viola-Cesario's appearance ('Not too fast! Soft, soft!')
- constantly beseeches Viola-Cesario to visit her
- marries Sebastian without recognising he is not Viola-Cesario
- equates love with sickness ('Even so quickly may one catch the plague?').

But in his portrayal of Olivia, Shakespeare balances her self-deceptions against her evident qualities. She is a capable mistress of her household, and possesses a wry humour. Towards the play's end she expresses concern for Malvolio's well-being ('poor gentleman'), and recognises that she too has been in the grip of 'A most extracting frenzy'.

Feste: a fool, but no fool

Fools were often employed in the palaces of royalty and great houses of noble families. Although they had the title of 'fool' (or jester or clown), they were much more intelligent than foolish ('a witty fool'). Their job was not simply to provide amusement, but to comment critically on contemporary behaviour. An 'allowed fool' was able to say what he thought. No punishment would follow: 'There is no slander in an allowed fool'.

Feste is such an 'allowed fool'. He is an emblem of the folly that runs through the play. He is employed by Olivia, and was a favourite of her father. He gets on well with Sir Toby, and is just as much at home at Duke Orsino's. Moving freely between Olivia's household and Orsino's palace, he links the love plot and the comic plots of the play. Only Malvolio dislikes him, and Feste extracts revenge on the puritanical steward.

Feste delights in wordplay. He puns, riddles, engages in repartee, invents mock-logical arguments, and seizes any opportunity to create nonsense from words. His language demonstrates how meanings shift constantly in the topsy-turvy world of Illyria.

Feste and Olivia. In many modern productions, Feste has been played as
troubled and morose rather than as merry. And Olivia is often portrayed as
responding with reserve to Feste's humour. But in this production Feste was
always cheerful and Olivia quickly abandoned her mourning and whole-
heartedly enjoyed his joking. Use the information on page 160 and the
illustrations to write your own pen portrait of one of these characters.

Malvolio

'O you are sick of self-love, Malvolio'. Olivia's accusation sums up the traditional view of Malvolio: that he

- is highly critical of people below him
- is disdainful towards Viola when returning the ring
- is intolerant of Sir Toby's merrymaking
- has secret fantasies that Olivia loves him
- has a self-conceit that causes him to fall easily into the trap set for him
- does not realise how ridiculous he looks, smiling and cross-gartered
- cannot forgive, but thinks only of revenge.

Malvolio represents a puritan killjoy disapproval of 'cakes and ale' festivity. His fantasies, conceit and sense of superiority bring him low as he is deceived by the forged letter. Like other characters, Malvolio is a dramatic portrayal of the folly that arises from delusion. But in spite of his arrogance, pomposity and lack of humour (and the implications of his name, Malvolio = 'ill-wishing'), he is an efficient and conscientious steward. His humiliating treatment as a madman often makes modern audiences feel uncomfortable.

Sir Toby Belch and Sir Andrew Aguecheek

Sir Toby Belch and Sir Andrew Aguecheek link the love plot and the comic plots. They are recognisable characters in dramatic tradition. Sir Toby represents the boastful, drunken braggart. His name, Belch, suggests his earthy nature. His behaviour displays the spirit of Twelfth Night: pleasure-seeking revelling ('cakes and ale') and the rejection of constraint (see p. 172).

Sir Andrew is the traditional 'gull', a rich ninny whose foolishness ensures that he is easily fleeced of his money by Sir Toby. He has no chance of winning Olivia's love, and is another character in the grip of illusion. He thinks of himself as a lover, a scholar and a skilled duellist, but each self-perception is comically exposed as a delusion.

Sir Toby is a bully, a cheat, a liar, and a cruel practical joker. He is also, like Malvolio, a hypocrite, because for all his anti-authoritarian revelling he is acutely conscious of his own social position as a relative of the high-status Olivia. But he is also brave and witty, and his melancholy echoes Orsino's. And Sir Andrew, for all his witlessness, has one of the most endearing lines in the play, which suggests he is yet another melancholy lover: 'I was adored once, too.'

'This is my lady's hand'. In this modern-dress production, Malvolio is
deceived by the forged letter. Fabian, Sir Andrew and Sir Toby watch from the
box hedge (for other portrayals of this 'overhearing' scene, see pictures on
pp. ix, 62, 69, 125 and 178).

♦ Use the information opposite as your starting point for an essay
 analysing the character of *either* Malvolio *or* Sir Toby.

The language of *Twelfth Night*

Imagery

Twelfth Night is full of imagery: words or phrases which conjure up emotionally laden pictures or associations in the mind. When Maria says 'here comes the trout that must be caught with tickling', her image is of Malvolio, who can be trapped by flattery, just as a fish can be teased into being caught. Similarly, when Antonio says that his desire 'More sharp than filèd steel, did spur me forth', his image vividly suggests the piercing and painful nature of his feelings for Sebastian which force him to follow him.

Shakespeare's imagery gives pleasure as it stirs the audience's imagination, deepens the dramatic impact of particular moments or moods, provides insight into character, and intensifies meaning and emotional force. Sir Toby paints a hilarious picture of Sir Andrew's cowardice: 'if he were opened and you find so much blood in his liver as will clog the foot of a flea, I'll eat the rest of th'anatomy'.

The Elizabethan world provides much of the play's imagery. For example, when Malvolio thinks he has truly captured Olivia's affection, he says, 'I have limed her'. The image is from the cruel practice of trapping birds with sticky lime spread on tree branches. Elsewhere, animals and birds provide a rich source of images. Sir Andrew has 'dormouse valour', Fabian says Viola 'looks pale, as if a bear were at his heels', and Orsino angrily describes Viola as a 'dissembling cub'.

All Shakespeare's imagery uses metaphor, simile or personification. All are comparisons which in effect substitute one thing (the image) for another (the thing described).

A **simile** compares one thing to another using 'like' or 'as'. Sir Toby says that Sir Andrew's hair 'hangs like flax on a distaff'. Orsino recalls Antonio's face in the sea-battle: 'it was besmeared / As black as Vulcan' (the Roman god of fire, blacksmith to the gods).

A **metaphor** is also a comparison, suggesting that two dissimilar things are actually the same. When Viola speaks of 'that orbèd continent the fire / That severs day from night' it is an elaborate description of the sun. Elsewhere, Sir Toby's image of 'cakes and ale' is a striking metaphor for a whole world of celebration, festivity and hedonistic enjoyment.

To put it another way, a metaphor borrows one word or phrase to express another. When, at the play's end, Feste says, 'And thus the whirligig of time brings in his revenges', his image is of a roundabout or child's whipping top, and the 'wheel of Fortune', suggesting that time brings about the revenge on Malvolio that Feste has long wished for.

Personification turns all kinds of things into persons, giving them human feelings or attributes. Viola personifies Patience in a vivid description of the effects of love that uses all three kinds of imagery:

> She never told her love,
> But let concealment like a worm i'th'bud
> Feed on her damask cheek. She pined in thought,
> And with a green and yellow melancholy
> She sat like Patience on a monument,
> Smiling at grief.
>
> *Act 2 Scene 4, lines 106–11*

Classical mythology contributes to the richness of the play's imagery. Elizabethans were more familiar with such references than are most members of audiences today. In the play's first scene they would recognise that Orsino's image of being turned into a deer pursued by savage hounds comes from a story in Ovid's *Metamorphoses*. The hunter Actaeon saw the goddess Diana bathing. As punishment he was turned into a stag and chased and killed by his own hunting dogs.

Similarly, Elizabethans, knowing that Jove is a god famous for his exploits in love, would find it appropriate that Malvolio thanks Jove for helping him (as he mistakenly believes) win the love of Olivia. In the same way, they would appreciate the humorous inappropriateness of Sir Toby's calling the diminutive Maria Penthesilea (queen of the Amazons).

Many other images from Greek and Roman mythology occur in the play. You will find brief explanations of each at appropriate points in the script (on the pages shown): 'Elysium' (p. 4), 'Arion on the dolphin's back' (p. 6), 'Diana' (p. 18), 'Vulcan' (p. 128), 'Jove' (pp. 24, 62, 66 and 93), 'Mercury' (p. 22), 'Lucrece' (p. 62) and 'Lethe' (p. 112).

◆ Orsino's language in Act 1 Scene 1 contains a series of images which recur throughout the play: music, death, the sea, hunting, disease ('pestilence'), love and flowers. Choose one image, find as many uses of it in the play as you can, and work out a vivid and effective way of displaying your findings (e.g. in an illustrated 'spider diagram').

Antithesis

Antithesis is the opposition of words or phrases against each other. When Viola exclaims about Olivia, 'But if you were the devil, you are fair!', the word 'devil' stands in contrast to 'fair'. There is similar setting of word against word when Fabian, looking for forgiveness for the trick he and the others have played on Malvolio, hopes it 'May rather pluck on laughter than revenge' ('laughter' versus 'revenge').

Antithesis is one of Shakespeare's favourite language devices. He uses it extensively in all his plays. Why? Because antithesis powerfully expresses conflict through its use of opposites, and conflict is the essence of all drama. In *Twelfth Night*, conflict occurs in many forms: the formality of Orsino's elegant court versus the more relaxed household of Olivia; Malvolio's uptight puritanism versus Sir Toby's carefree revels; Olivia's resistance to Orsino's wooing; Viola's emotional struggle ('barful strife') as her love for Orsino clashes with her duty to act as his love messenger to Olivia.

Even more strikingly, throughout the play there are many conflicts of reality versus appearance: a girl mistaken for a boy, one twin for another, a forged letter for a true declaration of love. Nothing is quite what it seems in this play of mistaken identity. Viola's remark to the Captain 'that nature with a beauteous wall / Doth oft close in pollution', and her declaration to Olivia that 'I am not what I am', are just two antitheses that express the conflict between outward show and inward reality.

Antithesis intensifies the sense of conflict. In the 'duel' scene (Act 3 Scene 4) Viola, preferring peace to duelling, says she would 'rather go with sir priest than sir knight'. Antonio, mistaking Viola for Sebastian and feeling betrayed, vehemently exclaims, 'O how vile an idol proves this god!' Absurdly wooing Olivia, Malvolio dismisses Maria as unworthy of an answer: 'nightingales answer daws'.

Feste's deliberately confusing antitheses are reminders that the genre of *Twelfth Night* is comedy. Shakespeare therefore ensures that conflicts result in humour rather than, as in the histories and tragedies, in unhappiness and death, as when Sebastian declares Olivia 'betrothed both to a maid and man'.

◆ Collect as many examples of antithesis as you can. Write an extended essay showing how antithesis helps create a strong sense of both conflict and humour in *Twelfth Night*.

Verse and prose

About one third of the play is in verse and two-thirds in prose. Theatrical convention was that prose was used by comic and low-status characters. High-status characters spoke verse. 'Comic' scenes were written in prose (as were letters, like the one Maria forges to trick Malvolio), but audiences expected verse to be spoken in 'serious' scenes because verse was thought particularly suitable for lovers and for moments of high dramatic or emotional intensity.

Shakespeare used his judgement about which conventions he should follow in *Twelfth Night*, and it is obvious that he often broke the 'rules'. Viola (high-status) switches frequently from verse to prose, and her first dialogue with Olivia (also high-status) is in prose. Sir Toby and Sir Andrew always use prose. They, too, are high-status characters, but their dramatic function is comic.

The verse of *Twelfth Night* is mainly 'blank verse' (unrhymed verse written in iambic pentameter). Iambic pentameter is a rhythm or metre in which each line has five stressed syllables (/) alternating with five unstressed syllables ($\times$):

$$\times \quad / \quad \times \quad / \quad \times \quad / \times \quad / \quad \times \quad /$$
O time, thou must untangle this, not I

♦ Choose a verse speech and speak it to emphasise the metre (five beats). Then speak it as you feel it should be delivered on stage. Finally, write four to eight lines of your own in the same style.
♦ Glance quickly at each scene in the play. Make a list showing which are mainly in verse, and which are mainly in prose. Suggest why.

Puns and wordplay

A pun is a play on words where the same sound has different meanings. Such playing with words was very popular in Shakespeare's time. In the opening scene, Orsino hears the word 'hart' (male deer) but plays with it as if it were 'heart'. Sir Toby first appears juggling with 'exceptions', 'except' and 'excepted', then with 'confine'. Feste's very first words pun on 'colours' (see p. 18), and he continues to play with words throughout *Twelfth Night*. Asked by Viola-Cesario, 'Dost thou live by thy tabor?', he replies, 'No, sir, I live by the church.' No wonder that Feste calls himself Olivia's 'corrupter of words'.

♦ Follow Feste through the play. Note each time he puns or riddles with words. Use your findings to write an essay titled 'How Feste's wordplay adds to the humour and mood of *Twelfth Night*'.

Illyria

Shakespeare's Illyria, a never-never land of make-believe and illusion, exists under many names: Utopia, the Big Rock Candy Mountain, fairyland, Xanadu, Arcadia, the Land of Cockaigne, Shangri-La, New Atlantis, Blue Remembered Hills, Dreamland. It is an enchanted world where happiness is truly possible; a fictitious world of romance, full of magical possibilities, thrilling and exotic, where anything can happen, but the result will be joy and harmony.

In other words, it's a state of mind, not the real, historical Illyria (see p. 34). It is a place which exists in the imagination, a realm in which characters are changed by experience. Shakespeare created similar worlds in his other plays: the Forest of Arden (*As You Like It*), the wood outside Athens (*A Midsummer Night's Dream*), Belmont (*The Merchant of Venice*), Ephesus (*The Comedy of Errors*). In these exotic locations of Shakespeare's comedies, confusions, errors and mistakes are made, but happiness and marriage result.

Illyria is a capricious world of disguise and mistaken identity. Language itself is unreliable – words slip and slide into confusion. Fantasy and everyday life rub shoulders – a fairy-tale duke inhabits the same world as the earthy Sir Toby Belch, a very English drunkard. Everything is untrustworthy and larger than life. Common sense is mocked, and nothing is quite what it seems. Folly abounds – one of the chief characters, Feste, is called 'the fool'. The threat of madness is common (the word 'mad' occurs more times in *Twelfth Night* than in any other play by Shakespeare). Much madness is to do with love, but Malvolio is almost driven to real madness.

But Illyria, for all its untrustworthiness, is a secure place. Brother finds sister; lovers will marry. Illusions are the way to find truth, and time will achieve a happy ending for most, but not all, of the characters. Some characters finish up with their heart's desire – or think they do.

The subtitle of the play, *What You Will*, was a common catchphrase in Shakespeare's time. Perhaps it says to the audience: 'make of it what you like, it's make-believe, but don't take it too seriously, because nothing is of consequence'.

A modern Illyria? Disney World, where fantasy rules.

Create your own Illyria

◆ Make a display (a collage, photomontage, or other illustration) to show your view of Illyria. Include quotations from the play.

◆ 'There's no such place as Illyria.'
'Oh yes there is!'
Take sides and argue for each claim.

169

Illyria: Shakespeare's England

Like all writers, Shakespeare reflected in his plays the world he knew. Illyria sounds like a far-away place – Orsino, Antonio and Malvolio are 'un-English' names (unlike Sir Toby, Sir Andrew and 'Mistress Mary'). But *Twelfth Night* is full of the customs, sights and sounds of Elizabethan England:

Hunting and field sports hounds, bird-bolts, beagle, stone-bow, staniel, cold scent, sowter, fox, haggard, feather, woodcock, gin, unmuzzled, whipstock.

Eating and drinking buttery-bar, canary, sack, beef (thought to make Englishmen stupid), alehouse, tosspots, pickled herring.

Songs and dances jig, galliard, coranto, caper, back-trick, sink-a-pace, catch, cantons, tabor, 'hold thy peace', 'Farewell dear heart'.

The countryside squash, peascod, codling, turkey-cock, dormouse, grey capilet, oxen and wainropes, bawcock, chuck, biddy, sheriff's post, orchard, box-tree.

Familiar words or phrases It's all one, Peg-a-Ramsey, cudgel, leman (sweetheart), cheveril glove, westward ho, the old Vice, asshead, coxcomb, knave, gull, what you will, coz, swabber, sneck up.

Occupations coziers, tinkers, weavers, stewards, spinsters (who spin flax on a distaff), knitters, grand jurymen, bumbailey, master crowner (coroner), parson, curate, Dick Surgeon, coistrill, groom.

Current affairs puritan, Brownist, yeoman of the wardrobe, Mistress Mall's picture, Lady of the Strachy, Dutchman's beard, the new map of the Indies, the sophy.

Places and customs south suburbs, the Elephant, St Bennet, the great bed of Ware, parish top, inventories, tray-trip, cherry-pit, acqua-vitae, bear-baiting.

Clothes gaskins, points, changeable taffeta, branched velvet gown, yellow stockings, cross-gartered.

Maria and Sir Toby Belch. Many productions of *Twelfth Night* costume the actors in the dress of Shakespeare's time. The play is set in Illyria, but Sir Toby in doublet and hose looks very much like an Elizabethan Englishman. Use this picture and the information on page 170 to compile an assignment (including illustrations and quotations) on 'How *Twelfth Night* reveals Shakespeare's England'.

171

Twelfth Night

In Elizabethan times, the twelve days after Christmas up to Twelfth Night on 6 January (Epiphany) were traditionally a time of holiday and festival. It was a time for celebration and revelry, sometimes known as the 'Feast of Fools'. All kinds of folly, pranks and deceptions were allowed in this period of high jinks, a topsy-turvy time of confusion and masquerades. A never-never land was created, remote from the every-day world. Normal behaviour and conventions could be suspended, and common sense and decorum went out of the window as people were released from their everyday inhibitions. Comedy and carnival, disguise and boisterous frivolity were the order of the day.

Authority was up-ended. For a short time, servants could order their masters about. Today, a relic of this tradition is the custom in the Army for officers to serve Christmas dinner to the soldiers. In universities, private houses and the Inns of Court (the law schools in London), a 'Lord of Misrule' was chosen (often a servant) who became, for a short period, master of the household. He (never she) organised dances, masques and make-believe activities.

But the major function of the twelve days was to remind the under-dogs where power really lay, and that the normal hierarchy would and must be obeyed after the short holiday. Twelfth Night itself marked the end of both the Christmas holiday and the holiday season. The next day it was back to the normality of hard work in the everyday world. The short time of pleasure was over. So 6 January was tinged with sadness, as the Christmas decorations were taken down and the festivities ended.

◆ Write about what might happen if a 'Lord of Misrule' was elected for a day in your school or college. What would you do if you were elected?

◆ Research modern periods of festivity such as the Notting Hill Carnival, *mardi gras* festivals in New Orleans and Rio de Janeiro, and the Munich *Oktoberfest*. Present your findings as an assignment, showing how far you think each is like the Feast of Fools.

The Bean-King (detail) by Jacob Jordaens (1642). The custom of appointing a Lord of Misrule from Christmas Day to Twelfth Night was widespread in Europe for many centuries. Its origins lay in the Saturnalia of ancient Rome, a time when slaves and masters changed places, and a mock king ruled a topsy-turvy world. At the Universities of Oxford and Cambridge, he was known as 'King of the Kingdom of the Bean', a title also used in Holland and Germany. When the University of Cambridge unsuccessfully tried to suppress the Bean-King and his revelry in 1646, 'some grave Governors mentioned the good use thereof, because thereby, in twelve days, they more discover the dispositions of Scholars than in twelve months before'.

Twelfth Night in performance

Sometime during 1600 and 1601 William Shakespeare, already well known as a successful playwright, wrote *Twelfth Night*. The dates are certain for two reasons. First, because Maria's comment about 'the new map with the augmentation of the Indies' (Act 3 Scene 2, lines 62–3) refers to a map of India and the Far East published in 1599. Second, because there is a record of a performance of the play on 2 February 1602. John Manningham, a lawyer, wrote about a performance he saw at the Middle Temple, one of London's Inns of Court (see picture opposite). Part of his diary entry reads:

> At our feast we had a play called 'Twelve Night, or What You Will'. . . A good practise in it to make the Steward believe his Lady widow was in love with him, by counterfeiting a letter as from his Lady in general terms, telling him what she liked best in him, and prescribing his gesture in smiling, his apparel, etc., and then when he came to practise making him believe they took him to be mad.

Manningham thought the play was much like Shakespeare's *The Comedy of Errors*, which also involves shipwrecked twins and mistaken identity.

Shakespeare probably took the idea of his play from an English adaptation of an Italian story, but he made significant alterations. In the original, the Sea Captain was a villain, Viola was imprisoned by the duke, and Olivia had a child by Sebastian. Shakespeare invented the Sir Toby subplot. In creating Viola-Cesario, he drew on his earlier plays in which women dressed as men (*Two Gentlemen of Verona*, *The Merchant of Venice*, *As You Like It*).

Right from the play's first performance, Malvolio seized the imagination of audiences. In 1632, King Charles I wrote 'Malvolio' against the title of the play in the collection of Shakespeare's plays which he owned. In 1640, Leonard Digges praised Shakespeare in verses which included the following lines testifying to Malvolio's box-office appeal:

> lo in a trice
> The Cockpit Galleries, Boxes, all are full
> To hear Malvolio that cross gartered Gull.

Perhaps Malvolio's revenge is that he has turned out to be the best-remembered character in the play!

In 1660, the diarist Samuel Pepys saw the play three times. He thought it 'silly', and could not see the point of the title. The play fell from favour for almost eighty years after Pepys saw it, but other playwrights repeatedly drew on it as a source of ideas and language for their own plays.

After its revival in 1741, *Twelfth Night* became increasingly popular. Many leading actors chose to play Malvolio. His 'darkened room' scene was played in a range of styles from tragedy to farce. In the nineteenth century, it became fashionable to add musical scenes filled with spectacle and festivity – some productions were virtually operas. Sebastian, Olivia and Viola often sang, and Viola was sometimes played like a hearty and enthusiastic principal boy in a pantomime. The whole company would join in a song and dance at the play's end. One production included two shipwreck scenes, and opened with fishermen and peasants singing 'Come unto these yellow sands' from *The Tempest*. In another, Orsino and Viola married in Illyria's cathedral.

Modern productions have moved away from elaborate spectacle. The concern has been to explore the play's complex moods through close attention to language and characterisation. Old conventions have

In 2002, exactly 400 years after John Manningham saw *Twelfth Night* in the Middle Temple, the Globe Theatre Company staged its own production there.

been reassessed: for example, in contrast with nineteenth-century productions, Olivia is now often played as a young woman, and Feste as a much older fool. There have been novel readings of the character Malvolio. One Malvolio left the stage apparently intent on suicide. Another gave his final words such evil undertones that it completely changed the comic mood. Yet another Malvolio bore a striking resemblance to Shakespeare.

Many modern productions stress the autumnal, elegiac mood of the play (see p. 153). They suggest that fertility and romantic idyll will soon give way to decay and winter. There is a growing trend for modern productions to portray Illyria as a society undergoing change. So Illyria is set as a feudal, male-dominated society, exercising control through licensed foolery. But it is threatened by a more modern, efficient society, characterised by the 'new man', the self-made, humourless Malvolio. He is impatient with the old order, and intolerant of fun and festivity. Such productions tend to see the play as giving a forewarning of the struggles to come, in the English Civil War of 1642–60 and the closure of the theatres.

Twelfth Night at the Globe

In Shakespeare's lifetime, *Twelfth Night* was performed at the Middle Temple (see pp. 174–5) and at the **Globe**, a round theatre open to the sky. The audience standing in the pit, the 'groundlings', got wet if it rained. Those in the galleries (who paid more) and the actors on stage were protected from the weather.

In Shakespeare's day, Viola, Olivia and Maria were played by boys. There were no elaborate sets on the bare stage of the Globe, but the actors dressed in attractive and expensive costumes, usually the fashionable dress of the times. Only a few props were used: a table, chairs, swords and tankards, and perhaps a 'box-tree' behind which Sir Toby and the others hid to overhear Malvolio reading the letter.

The Globe Theatre has now been rebuilt on London's Bankside, close to the site on which it first stood. Many of its productions are staged as Shakespeare's Elizabethan and Jacobean audiences probably saw them. In 2002 the Globe's production of *Twelfth Night* was staged in that way. All the female parts were played by men, and the play was performed in Elizabethan costumes.

◆ Write an essay which analyses the dramatic advantages and disadvantages of performing *Twelfth Night* with an all-male (or all-female) cast.

Mark Rylance as Olivia in the Globe's all-male production, which played at Middle Temple exactly 400 years after the play's first recorded performance there. Olivia was dignified, with a quiet sense of humour, but very determined – she prevented the duel between Sebastian and Sir Toby by rushing on with a 12-foot spear!

Overhearing Malvolio. This production emphasised the 'Twelfth Night' aspect of the play with the conspirators hiding behind a Christmas tree to eavesdrop on Malvolio (see also pictures on pp. ix, 62, 69 and 163).

The imprisonment of Malvolio can be a cruel episode. Here, he was quite literally caged behind bars (see also pictures on pp. xi (bottom) and 118) and taunted by Feste, pretending to be Sir Topas.

Twelfth Night is a favourite play for open-air productions. Compare this picture of Malvolio showing off his yellow stockings and cross-garters with the pictures on pages x, 90 and 125. Then compile an assignment (a file of drawings, notes and suggestions, a website, or an active presentation) setting out your ideas for your own production (think about set design, costumes, a publicity poster, a programme and character notes).

William Shakespeare
1564–1616

1564   Born Stratford-upon-Avon, eldest son of John and Mary Shakespeare.

1582   Marries Anne Hathaway of Shottery, near Stratford.

1583   Daughter, Susanna, born.

1585   Twins, son and daughter, Hamnet and Judith, born.

1592   First mention of Shakespeare in London. Robert Greene, another playwright, described Shakespeare as 'an upstart crow beautified with our feathers . . .'. Greene seems to have been jealous of Shakespeare. He mocked Shakespeare's name, calling him 'the only Shake-scene in a country' (presumably because Shakespeare was writing successful plays).

1595   A shareholder in The Lord Chamberlain's Men, an acting company that became extremely popular.

1596   Son Hamnet dies, aged 11.
       Father, John, granted arms (acknowledged as a gentleman).

1597   Buys New Place, the grandest house in Stratford.

1598   Acts in Ben Jonson's *Every Man in His Humour*.

1599   Globe Theatre opens on Bankside. Performances in the open air.

1601   Father, John, dies.

1603   James I grants Shakespeare's company a royal patent: The Lord Chamberlain's Men become The King's Men and play about twelve performances each year at court.

1607   Daughter, Susanna, marries Dr John Hall.

1608   Mother, Mary, dies.

1609   The King's Men begin performing indoors at Blackfriars Theatre.

1610   Probably returns from London to live in Stratford.

1616   Daughter, Judith, marries Thomas Quiney.
       Dies. Buried in Holy Trinity Church, Stratford-upon-Avon.

The plays and poems
(no one knows exactly when he wrote each play)

1589–95   *The Two Gentlemen of Verona, The Taming of the Shrew, First, Second and Third Parts of King Henry VI, Titus Andronicus, King Richard III, The Comedy of Errors, Love's Labour's Lost, A Midsummer Night's Dream, Romeo and Juliet, King Richard II* (and the long poems *Venus and Adonis* and *The Rape of Lucrece*).

1596–9   *King John, The Merchant of Venice, First and Second Parts of King Henry IV, The Merry Wives of Windsor, Much Ado About Nothing, King Henry V, Julius Caesar* (and probably the *Sonnets*).

1600–5   *As You Like It, Hamlet, Twelfth Night, Troilus and Cressida, Measure for Measure, Othello, All's Well That Ends Well, Timon of Athens, King Lear*.

1606–11   *Macbeth, Antony and Cleopatra, Pericles, Coriolanus, The Winter's Tale, Cymbeline, The Tempest*.

1613   *King Henry VIII, The Two Noble Kinsmen* (both probably with John Fletcher).

1623   Shakespeare's plays published as a collection (now called the First Folio).